AWAY WITH THE GATEKEEPERS

DAN THOMPSON

AWAY WITH THE GATEKEEPERS

SOCIAL MEDIA AS A TOOL FACILITATING NONVIOLENT STRUGGLE DURING THE 2011 EGYPTIAN REVOLUTION

DAN THOMPSON BOOKS

Boston • Charleston • Frankfurt • Kathmandu • London • Seoul

Away with the Gatekeepers:
Social Media as a Tool Facilitating Nonviolent Struggle
During the 2011 Egyptian Revolution

and

The Tweet Heard Around the World: The Growing Influence of the
Multinational New Media Industry in International Relations

ISBN 13: ISBN-13: 978-1481890823   ISBN-10: 1481890824

This research was presented and defended on July 19, 2012 at the Fletcher
School of Law and Diplomacy, Tufts University, Medford, Massachusetts.
It has not been extensively peer reviewed and should be considered as
preliminary research meant to inform greater discussion on the topic and
further advanced research.

The opinions and positions expressed are the author's and the author's
alone and do not represent the opinions of the Fletcher School, the
U.S. Government or the North Atlantic Treaty Organization.

Printed in the United States of America

For Nora, Gene, Jamila & Dalia

#Jan25

Abstract

In the wake of the January 25, 2011 Revolution in Egypt there has been much speculation in Western media about the role social media played in bringing down Hosni Mubarak after 30 years of autocratic rule, many even going so far as to call it a "Facebook revolution." This paper argues that social media greatly enhanced Egyptian nonviolent struggle and political defiance as defined by nonviolent struggle theorists Gene Sharp and Peter Ackerman, in particular by enabling coordinated mass action, decentralization of leadership structure, creation of alternative media and social structures, all of which are key aspects of successful nonviolent struggle. This paper will attempt to demonstrate how social media successfully complimented nonviolent struggle in the 2011 Egyptian Revolution.

This is an exciting time to be in the public affairs and international relations field as social media has begun to influence public policy not just in the United States, but also around the world. The idea for this thesis was born one night in 2009 in Seoul, South Korea during the Iranian Green Revolution. I stayed up until early in the morning glued to a Twitter stream populated by Iranian revolutionaries and recalled how similar their live "tweets" were to combat reports that I processed in Baghdad, Iraq from 2003-2004 as a soldier in a command center. I then realized quite clearly that social media was more than just fancy e-mail. It was going to allow individuals the unprecedented ability to act in unison with others with military-like coordination…and quite possibly change the world for better *and* worse.

This thesis is a modest attempt to explore how social media may have helped coordinate nonviolent struggle in the 2011 Egyptian Revolution. It remains my hope that social media can be used for good, giving a voice to those yearning for expression and nonviolent collective action. But more importantly, this thesis seeks to explain that successful movements need more than just people power. They need a strategy. In this case and others, the successful application of strategic nonviolent struggle has been key to bringing down oppressive governments and enemies of freedom while avoiding bloody conflict that has all too often stained mankind for millennia. It is my hope that policy makers and those in diplomacy and defense will come to see nonviolent struggle theories, pioneered by Gene Sharp, as highly effective, if not equal or superior to, alternatives to armed conflict and occupation.

THIS THESIS IS DEDICATED IN MEMORY
OF KHALED SAID, KILLED IN 2010
BY EGYPTIAN SECRET POLICE
FOR SEEKING THE TRUTH.

Table of Contents

1. Introduction   3
    What is nonviolent struggle?
    What is social media?
    Social Media Use in Egypt
        What is Facebook?
        What is YouTube?
        What is Twitter?

2. Nonviolent movements in Egypt before January 25, 2011   10

3. Theories on Nonviolent Struggle & Strategies   11
        Key Sharp Theories
        Key Ackerman Theories

4. Methodology   16

5. Case Study: January 25, 2011 Egyptian Revolution   17
        Facebook and the January 25 Revolution
        YouTube and the January 25 Revolution
        Twitter and the January 25 Revolution

6. Analysis   36

7. Conclusions and Recommendations   48

Bibliography   54

Appendices
    Appendix A: Egyptian Facebook Screen Captures   59
    Appendix B: Egyptian YouTube Screen Captures   61
    Appendix C: Egyptian Twitter Screen Captures   63
    Appendix D: January 25 Protest Declaration on Google Documents 67
    Appendix E: 198 Nonviolent Weapons   77
    Appendix F: Blueprint of Social Media in 2011 Egyptian Revolution 81
    Appendix G: Channeling negative sentiment into action   82

The Tweet Heard Around the World: The Growing Influence of the   83
Multinational New Media Industry in International Relations (2009 essay)

Aknowledgements   91

List of Figures

Fig. 1   The social web diagram   5

Fig. 2   "We are all Khaled Said" protest event page   18

Fig. 3   Khaled Said Facebook photomontage   20

Fig. 4   Photo of positive civilian authority interaction   22

Fig. 5   Activist Asmaa Mahfouz   23

Fig. 6   A sketch showing protestors where to gather   24

Fig. 7   Video memorializing Khaled Said   25

Fig. 8   Video of a young boy leading protest chants   26

Fig. 9   Twitter user shares a nonviolent tactic   30

Fig. 10   Projectile labeled "Made in the USA"   33

Fig. 11   Photos of pro-Mubarak protest   34

Fig. 12   "We are all Khaled Said Facebook page   59

Fig. 13   "We are all Khaled Said" protest guidance   60

Fig. 14   April 6 Youth Movement Facebook page   62

Fig. 15   Video of protesters going to Tahrir Square   62

Fig. 16   Dalia Ziada discussing the use of violence   61

Fig. 17   Activist links to the January 25 manifesto   61

Fig. 18   Photos of pro-Mubarak protest   62

Fig. 19   Twitter photo of ammunition   65

Fig. 20   Twitter photo of protesters   66

Fig. 21   Twitter post reporting on police behavior   66

"Technology is neither good nor bad. Nor is it neutral" ~ Melvin Kranzberg

التكنولوجيا ليست جيدة أو سيئة. كما أنها ليست محايدة

1. Introduction

A digital media revolution is underway that is changing the way people around the globe consume and share information. Social networking sites like Facebook and Twitter are allowing users to share everything from family recipes to plans to overthrow governments – in real time. As Egyptians crowded into Tahrir Square on January 25, 2011, some carrying signs emblazoned with Facebook and Twitter logos (Michaels 2011), Western news media began asking a question that became a reoccurring theme on primetime news and Sunday morning talk shows in the United States: Did social media cause the nonviolent revolution in Egypt, and was it the invisible hand behind the Arab Spring movement? Indeed, an ongoing debate has erupted onto the pages of the *New Yorker* and *Foreign Affairs* magazine between cyber utopians like New York University professor Clay Shirky (Shirky 2010) and skeptics such as best-selling author Malcolm Gladwell (Gladwell 2010) as to whether social media was a deciding factor in creating grassroots change.

This paper will not attempt to answer the question of whether or not social media *caused* a nonviolent revolution in Egypt, but it will seek to investigate the following:

- Was there a substantive link between social media and the January 25, 2011 Egyptian nonviolent struggle?
- Did the use of social media in the January 25 revolution complement the principle characteristics of nonviolent conflict?

In this paper, the author will first establish what nonviolent struggle is and outline its core features. Second, the author will define what social media consists of according to industry standards. Third, the author will discuss theories of nonviolent struggle. Fourth, the author will make three hypotheses regarding the relationship between nonviolent movements and social media. Fifth, the author will present a case study including observations about social media and nonviolent movement interaction in the January 25 revolution in Egypt extracted from news articles, interviews, and other sources. Sixth, an analysis will apply the theory and test the hypotheses. Finally, the author will discuss conclusions and recommendations.

What is Nonviolent Struggle?

Nonviolent struggle is an umbrella term created and preferred by one of the world's leading theorists on nonviolent action, Gene Sharp (2007). Other terms for nonviolent struggle also include nonviolent action, nonviolent conflict, and political defiance (Sharp 2007). This paper will use the terms interchangeably.

According to the International Center on Nonviolent Conflict (ICNC), nonviolent struggle is the active, strategic application of civilian methods of resistance to oppressive government power. This is unlike *nonviolence*, which involves varying degrees of pacifism based on moral values ("What is it" 2009). The ICNC states that nonviolent conflict seeks to undermine official power by allowing participants to "withdraw their cooperation from an oppressive system by using tactics such as strikes, boycotts, and mass protests" ("Basic Concepts" 2009). Because members become less active in the institutions of the state, they begin to establish their own forums of parallel influence, and thus power (Wheeler 2008).

The creation of alternative forms of power is a key feature of nonviolent conflict. German sociologist Max Weber defined power as the "ability of an actor to realize his or her will in a social action, even against the will of other actors" (Shortell 2003). Nonviolent conflict methods allow for the expression of personal will in social behavior despite state controls. According to ICNC, some of those behaviors may include sit-ins, boycotts, mass demonstrations, and more than 198 other options detailed in Appendix E (ICNC 2009). Theories on nonviolent struggle will be detailed in the Nonviolent Struggle Theory chapter of this paper, focusing on theorists Gene Sharp and Peter Ackerman.

What is Social Media?

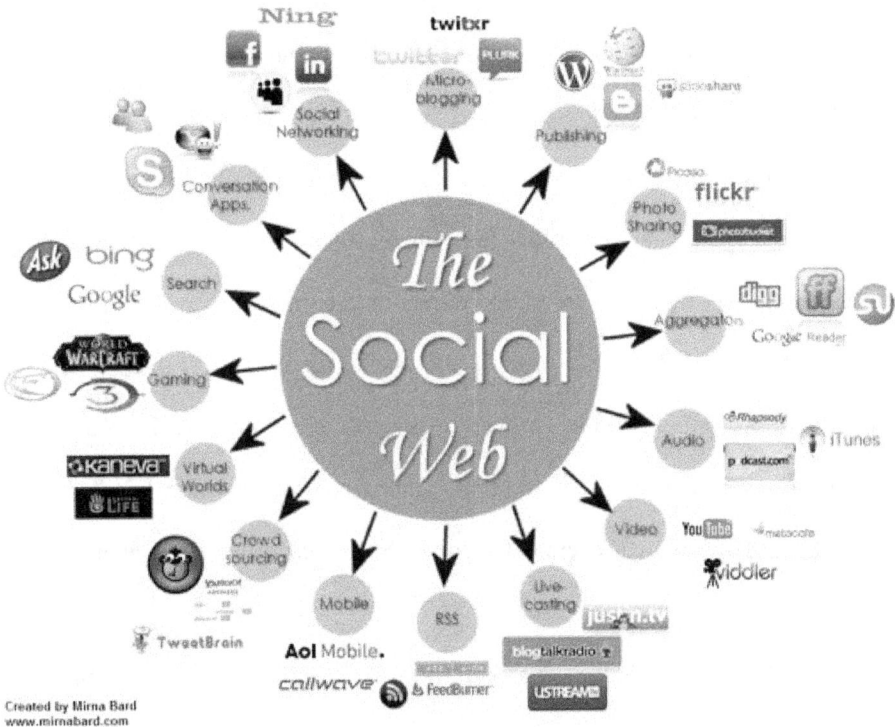

Fig. 1 An example of social media tools commonly used in the globalized Internet communications setting.

The term *Social Media* is constantly evolving. In the *Journal of Computer-Mediated Communication,* scholars Danah M. Boyd and Nicole B. Ellison as "web-based services that allow individuals to (1) construct a public or semi-public profile within a bounded system, (2) articulate a list of other users with whom they share a connection, and (3) view and traverse their list of connections and those made by others within the system. The nature and nomenclature of these connections may vary from site to site" (Boyd and Ellison 2008).

Understanding what social media is also requires an understanding of the categories of social media and the tools used to propagate it. There are approximately 15 categories of social media platforms in existence (*see Fig. 1*), with Facebook, YouTube and Twitter being among the most recognizable brands in the world and also in Egypt (Fattah 2008). For this reason, this paper will focus on these three main platforms.

A fundamental characteristic of each platform is its instant two-way communications ability and free or low cost. Unlike traditional news websites, social media allows users to rapidly share information with their networks with a click of a mouse and express their sentiment towards an issue by commenting, rating an item, or a combination of both (Rugh 2008). This creates a ripple effect, or viral, mode of communication that transmits ideas and sentiment more efficiently than targeted, single addressee e-mails, traditional letters to the editor, SMS messaging, and telephone calls (Clay 2011).

As a two-way communications platform, social media is unlike traditional one-way broadcast media such as radio and television in that it needs inputs from users to be truly social. A minimum set of specific tools is needed to populate social media. Those tools include a personal computer, laptop computer, tablet computer, handheld device (like a web-enabled iPod), cell phone, or smartphone, all of which will require an internet connection to communicate with the social web (Howard 2010). Many of these devices contain built-in video and photography capability. Access to the Internet may be provided by a local Internet service provider through physical infrastructure in a home or office, wireless cell phone modem, or satellite Internet connection (Philip 2010, 141-2). Additionally, the devices and underlying infrastructure also require a power source to operate.

Social Media Use in Egypt

According to media researcher Rasha Abdulla, basic access to Internet and infrastructure has been available relatively liberally in Egypt since 1996 (Abdulla 2005). Indeed, Egypt has the highest number of Facebook users in the Arab world, with the most popular social media services in Egypt being Facebook and YouTube, with Twitter growing in popularity (Fattah 2008). Currently, 14.09% of all Egyptians are registered on Facebook, or put another way, 66.48% of Egyptians with Internet access have Facebook accounts (Egypt Facebook Statistics). Theoretically, any Egyptian with Internet access may also access Facebook as an unregistered user.

What is Facebook?

Facebook is a web and mobile-based social media platform that allows users to connect to other individual users (called "friends"), groups, and organizations to share text messages, photos, videos, and event schedules online. It represents the fusion of e-mail, online photo sharing, texting, telephony, and calendar sharing that had earlier been compartmentalized into different, unsynchronized services (International Communication Association 2005).

Facebook users can add other users to their circle of online "friends" by sending requests to other users. The more friends one has, the greater their virtual online reach may become because of the increased visibility of content. Facebook users may also create or join a group, which is simply a virtual assembly of people who may have like interests, but are not necessarily "friends" on Facebook. Here, members may contribute content to a group, such as photos and videos, documents, comments, and events. The more members a group has, the wider the content is distributed. This makes Facebook group pages ideal for organizations, fan clubs, and other entities needing to share information and experiences without becoming "friends" with each member of the group, and thus retaining some digital privacy. Some common uses of group and organization pages include celebrity pages, politics (members of congress, campaigns), and product marketing (International Communication Association 2005, 129).

What is YouTube?

According to the *PC Magazine Encyclopedia,* YouTube is a video sharing website and mobile application that allows anyone with access to the Internet to upload, share, and view videos instantly from around the world. YouTube is social in that users may post content at will, comment on content instantly, and share content with others. They may even link these videos to Facebook and Twitter to extend the visibility of the content beyond that of YouTube ("Definition of YouTube" n.d.).

Unlike traditional broadcast media, YouTube requires only basic tools (at least a low-end digital camera) and has virtually no basic entry costs other than those associated with a personal computer or mobile device and Internet service. Additionally, anyone with access to the Internet may view public YouTube videos without being a registered YouTube user. Because of its ease of use, YouTube has become a repository for millions of amateur videos from around the globe. Traditional news services have recognized the value of being able to pull video, albeit in lesser quality, directly from areas impacted by major events such as unrest and natural disasters. Whereas major news companies once had to send journalists and film crews into places that may have taken hours or days to reach, they may now be able to augment their reporting with video uploaded on-site by people using YouTube. According to John Sutter of CNN, this has been the case in Syria where YouTube footage of attacks uploaded by people on-site has often been the only footage available to the outside world (Sutter 2012).

What is Twitter?

According to *PC Magazine Encyclopedia*, Twitter is a web and mobile application that allows users to post short, 140 character messages to the Internet, share links to photos and videos, and send direct message to other users ("Definition of Twitter n.d.). The content Twitter users generate are called "tweets." Twitter users are social in that they may follow other users, reply to or repost their tweets, and share tweets easily across many mediums, including Facebook. The Twitter interface is very simple and does not require high bandwidth to operate. Unlike SMS messaging on cell phones, Twitter allows for intuitive organization of messages and broader sharing possibilities not linked to cumbersome telephone numbers and pay-per-message costs. With a mobile or static Internet connection, one may send one, or thousands, of messages to the Internet where they may be read widely and further disseminated. It offers a rapidly scalable option to those looking to communicate with others ("Definition of Twitter " n.d.).

2. Nonviolent Movements in Egypt before January 25, 2011

Nonviolent struggle in Egypt has been taking place in one form or another for years in Egypt with limited success. Egyptian journalist and women's rights activist Mona Eltahawy points out that Egyptians have been nonviolently protesting against their government in Tahrir Square since the early 90s, but with the brunt of the anger directed at foreign policy (Arab American National Museum 2011). Examples include mass rallies against Operation Desert Storm and Mubarak's support for Israel in the 2006 war with Lebanon. Eltahawy says these were largely tolerated because they ultimately strengthened nationalism and pan Arab pride while not challenging the state's power (Arab American National Museum 2011). Nonviolent struggle has only recently gained more attention in the Western media as former U.S. ally Mubarak was ousted in what has been dubbed by some as the "Arab Spring" and "Egyptian Facebook Revolution." (Arab American National Museum 2011).

Egyptian civil disobedience became less predictable at the beginning of the 21st century, with an increasing number of youths being incarcerated (Fandy 2002). There are many theories surrounding what caused this increase in open political activity. Digital technologies sociologist Philip N. Howard posits that the wider availability of cell phones and Internet allowed Egyptians to compare outside political systems (Howard 2010) to their own and discuss them cheaply to a wider network (James 2001). Others cite the growing dissatisfaction of youths with little prospects for future prosperity in a system overburdened by corruption and joblessness, the fall of Saddam Hussein, which may have inspired in some Egyptians a belief that they too could free themselves from authoritarian power, and still others looked at the Muslim Brotherhood (Arab American National Museum 2011).

Whatever the causes, it is clear is that there has been an increase in Egyptian nonviolent struggle and the NGOs that plan them since 2000 (Ayyad 2009 , 90-104). Some of those NGOs are connected either directly or indirectly to pro-democracy efforts inspired by Gene Sharp. The successful Serbian nonviolent struggle movement OTPOR was founded in 1998 and its leaders met with Sharp in Budapest in 2000 in planning to undermine Slobodan Milosevic (Williams 2012). Seeing that movement as a possible template for other nonviolent movements, OPTOR activists Srdja Popovic and Slobodan Djinovic created Canvas, the Center for Applied Nonviolent Action and Strategies.

According to *The New York Times* (2006), pro-democracy NGOs like Canvas and the International Center for Nonviolent Conflict played an influential role in cross pollenating Sharp's ideas in Egypt and Tunisia leading up to the January 25, 2011 Revolution. In Egypt, activists from the April 6 Youth Movement and Dalia Ziada, among others, participated in workshops run by Canvas and the ICNC. In 2009, Egyptian activists, frustrated by their unsuccessful attempts at creating mass nonviolent struggle, flew to Serbia in 2009 for Canvas workshops on "organization, mobilization, overcoming fear and passivity, and training other protesters to spread the techniques" (Stolberg 2011). *The New York Times* also reports that Peter Ackerman facilitated a workshop on nonviolent struggle in Cairo "several years ago" (Stolberg 2011). While it is difficult to gauge the effectiveness of these efforts, in an interview with Gene Sharp, *Al Jazeera* reported that the Muslim Brotherhood had his book *From Dictatorship to Democracy* translated into Arabic on their website (Q&A: Gene Sharp 2011). The Muslim Brotherhood was one of the signers of the Google Document January 25 Protest Manifesto and they would later be elected to a majority government in Egypt in 2012.

3. Theories on Nonviolent Struggle & Strategies

Although literature on nonviolent struggle is not as comprehensive as that on armed conflict throughout history, a growing interest in nonviolent conflict has developed since the publication of Gene Sharp's *Politics of Nonviolent Action* in 1973 (wagingnonviolentstruggle.com). As one of the leading nonviolent struggle theorists and founder of the Albert Einstein Institute, his work was originally inspired by Gandhi's nonviolent struggle in India. In February 2011, *New York Times* journalist Sheryl Gay Stolberg wrote that Sharp's pamphlet *From Dictatorship to Democracy* had "inspired dissidents around the world, including in Burma, Bosnia, Estonia and Zimbabwe, and now Tunisia and Egypt" (Stolberg 2011).

Another influential theorist is an understudy of Sharp named Peter Ackerman, founding chair of the ICNC. Ackerman has further developed his own theories on nonviolent struggle based on Sharp's works and focused on providing the public with greater access to knowledge to inform their own nonviolent struggles. He has accomplished this by using multimedia like the ICNC's website, documentaries, and simulations. The ICNC website is a hub for case studies, workshops, and more, while films like "Bringing Down a Dictator" and "A Force More Powerful" demonstrate theory in practice, such as OTPOR's role in bringing down Serbia's Slobodan Milosevic in 2000 (Stolberg 2011).

Elements of both Sharp and Ackerman's theories on nonviolent struggle will be outlined below and used to analyze to what extent they may have been enhanced by social media in the January 25, 2011 Egyptian Revolution to bolster people power and help overthrow Egyptian dictator Hosni Mubarak.

Key Sharp Theories

In his work *Dictatorship to Democracy*, Sharp argues that oppressive governments have been able to prevent mass action by atomizing society so that it is "unable to work together to achieve freedom, to confide in each other, or even to do much of anything on their own initiative" (Sharp 2011). A key to weakening a dictatorship is generating mass action so that:

- The oppressed population themselves in their determination, self confidence, and resistance skills are strengthened.

- Independent social groups and institutions of oppressed people are created.

- A powerful internal resistance force is created.

- A wise grand strategic plan for liberation and implement it skillfully is developed (Sharp 2011, 12).

In order to accomplish these goals, Sharp identified 198 nonviolent "weapons" classified into three categories: protest and persuasion, noncooperation, and intervention all outlined in Appendix A (Sharp 2011, 46). When applied politically in a nonviolent struggle, these weapons become acts of *political defiance*, which implies more than merely noncooperation (Sharp 2011, 136). According to Sharp, political defiance has seven characteristics:

- It does not accept that the outcome will be decided by the means of fighting chosen by the dictatorship.

- It is difficult for the regime to combat.

- It can uniquely aggravate weakness of the dictatorship and can sever its sources of power.

- It can in action be widely dispersed but can also be concentrated on a specific objective.

- It leads to errors of judgment and action caused by the dictators.

- It can effectively utilize the population as a whole and the society's groups and institutions in the struggle to end the brutal domination of the few.

- It helps to spread the distribution of effective power in the society, making the establishment and maintenance of a democratic society more possible (Sharp 2011, 44).

In his work, *Waging Nonviolent Struggle*, Sharp writes that nonviolent struggles succeed because of at least one of four mechanisms: conversion, accommodation, nonviolent coercion, or disintegration (Sharp 2007, 46). Conversion means that the opponent is completely converted to the resisters' side, which is rare. Accommodation means that the opponent makes some key concessions to meet resisters' demands. Nonviolent coercion occurs when opponents are still in official positions, but possess no real power because the power structure is ignoring their commands and massive civil action can dictate terms to the opponent, as in Egypt in 2011. Disintegration is the complete collapse of a government with no one left to negotiate with (Sharp 2007, 47).

An overarching theme in Sharp's theories is his assertion that "in order to have a significant political impact, the disobedience and noncooperation often need to take the form of mass action. Acts of individuals may not have much impact, but the defiance of institutions can be pivotal as pillars of support" (Sharp 2007, 35).

Key Ackerman Theories

Ackerman focuses on a theoretical framework that identifies three essential pillars of successful nonviolent conflict: unity of movement, planning, and commitment to nonviolence (Ackerman 2010).

- *Unity of Movement*

The movement has a sense of shared purpose and realistic, attainable goals. According to Ackerman, central, a charismatic leadership figure like Martin Luther King, Jr. or Gandhi is not required (Ackerman 2010).

- *Planning*

The movement must be able to plan mobilization, tactics, and the sequence of action both defensively and offensively. In both modes, a movement must be able to anticipate the behavior of the opposing force, allocate appropriate resources, and react quickly to maximize its effect on the enemy (Ackerman 2010).

- *Nonviolent Discipline*

In order to remain a truly nonviolent conflict, participants must remain committed to nonviolent principles despite the temptation to resort to violence. Ackerman notes that nonviolent actors transitioning into armed fighters risk drawing the greater population into armed conflict and reduce the likelihood that opposing forces will be drawn to convert to the cause of the nonviolent movement (Ackerman 2010). Just as police and military forces exercise rules of engagement, nonviolent conflict actors also require their own rules of engagement to ensure uniformity of effort and to avoid broadening the scope of the crisis beyond what is manageable for the weaker party and lessen the likelihood of deadly force (2009).

4. Methodology

The research scope of this paper is focused on sources drawn from Egyptian activists, academic writings, media reports, and observations of online Egyptian social media such as Facebook, YouTube, and Twitter. The methodology of this paper will involve presenting three hypotheses that seek to establish a link between Sharp and Ackerman's theories of nonviolent struggle and social media, identifying indicators of each hypothesis, and testing them against a case study of the January 25, 2011 Egyptian Revolution and associated events.

1) *Social media was used in the 2011 Egyptian Revolution to promote unity of movement.*

The author hypothesizes that social media has and is being used to promote unity of the 2011 Egyptian Revolution nonviolent conflict actors. Because of the efficiency and speed of electronic communications, this may allow large groups of people to be informed in less time and with less expense than traditional paper media and telephones.

Indicators

1a) Social media was used to publicize agendas

1b) Social media was used to call people to mass action

1c) Social media was used to spread propaganda

2) *Social media was used as a planning tool*

The author hypothesizes that social media was used to quickly gather field intelligence, share it in real time with thousands of others, and share operational knowledge in order to help outmaneuver the Egyptian police.

Indicators

2a) Social media was used to collect field intelligence

2b) Social media was used to coordinate maneuvers

2c) Social media was used to share operational knowledge and lessons learned

3) ***Social media was used to promote nonviolent discipline***

The author hypothesizes that constant nonviolent conflict strategic messaging and the viral sharing of these messages was a factor in establishing an informal code of conduct amongst revolutionaries and maintaining discipline, not allowing the movement to become a civil war.

Indicators

3a) Codes of nonviolent conduct and values are embedded in communications

3b) The public openly publicizes their own acts of nonviolence

3c) Violent is rejected, instigators are confronted and publically shunned

5. Case Study: The January 25, 2011 Egyptian Revolution

Although nonviolent struggle has existed in Egypt in one form or another, the January 25, 2011 Revolution, now known as the 2011 Egyptian Revolution, represents the apogee of modern nonviolent struggle in Egypt to date. According to Jim Michaels of *USA Today*, January 25 is actually Police Day in Egypt (Michaels 2011), and was chosen as a day of protest by the Facebook page titled "We are all Khaled Said" (facebook.com/ElShaheeed). Khaled Said was an Egyptian blogger who was arrested on June 6, 2010 and killed by torture at the hands of the Egyptian police for possessing potentially damaging video implicating the police in dealing drugs. He was traced by secret police to an Internet café while using a computer there and beaten to death in retaliation. According to Ben Wederman of CNN, when Khaled's family visited the morgue to identify his body, Khaled's brother took a digital photo using his cell phone of his disfigured face and badly beaten body, which was later used as evidence by Human Rights Watch and former International Atomic Energy Agency Secretary General Mohamed Al-Baradei of President Hosni Mubarak's systematic use of torture. The image triggered a surge in social media activity that culminated with the "We are all Khaled Said" Facebook page being created, which then was used to launch a Facebook event calling for the January 25, 2011 protests.

Facebook and the January 25 Revolution

Fig. 2 The "We are all Khaled Said" page created an event that attracted 97,464 "attending" Facebook users. Such a very high number of attendees was thought to embolden protesters to attend (El Shaheeed 2011).

Of all of the social media available in Egypt, Facebook is ranked as the most popular and has the highest usage in the Arab world (*Globe and Mail* 2011). When the January 25 Revolution began, Egypt was estimated to have more than 3.4 million users, most of them less than 25 years old (*Globe and Mail* 2011). The most popular Egyptian Facebook protest page leading up to and during the January 25 Revolution was "We are all Khaled Said" in Arabic (كلنا خالد سعيد).[1] At the time of the revolution, "We are all Khaled Said" had more than 500,000 Arabic language followers. At the date of this paper's publication, it has 2,671,894 followers and more than 437,838 mentions on other Facebook pages.[2] Initially, it was reported that the protest page was organized by an anonymous entity (Giglio 2011), but later Google marketing executive and Egyptian Wael Ghonim was revealed as the page's creator. On January 28, he was arrested by the Egyptian police for activities unrelated to the page (Bradley 2011).

Posing an alternative to traditional and state-controlled media, the "We are all Khaled Said" Facebook protest page was created on June 10, 2010 with the purpose of exposing police corruption and systematic violence carried out by Hosni Mubarak under the Emergency Law (Emon, Lust and Macklin 2011). Using basic Facebook features, the site administrators and the public who had opted to join the site[3] could post photos and videos, links to outside media, schedule events, post notes, and more. The feature that proved most important on the "We are all Khaled Said" page was the event feature. Facebook allows users to create public and private events that other users can signal their intent to attend or not attend. The events feature was used to signal that a protest would take place on January 25, 2011, also known as Police Day in Egypt (see Fig. 2).

---

[1] The Arabic version Facebook page may be found at http://www.facebook.com/ElShaheeed. The Arabic
[2] Data collected directly from the site, http://www.facebook.com/ElShaheeed/likes
[3] Anyone with an Internet connection may view a public Facebook page. However, they must be a Facebook user and "Like" a page in order to publish material to a page.

The January 25 event page was more than a calendar invite, it was a dynamic coordination hub that in military terms may be called a "force multiplier." The page included a specific location (Tahrir Square), a time, and coordinating instructions. By clicking a link on the page, users could read a comprehensive document in the Notes section that stated in Arabic, "this page does not follow any party or group or movement or association…and do not support a person or idea…is for all Egyptians who want to defend their rights."[5] More specifically, it outlined specific demands on the government (minimum wage increase, term limits, student stipends, etc.), coordination times

Fig. 3 Example of Facebook photomontage that sparked strong public reaction and led to an increase in page followers worldwide.[4]

per neighborhood, standard chants, code of conduct, legal assistance phone numbers, and influential supporters of the demonstration (from the relatively liberal April 6 Youth Movement to the conservative Muslim Brotherhood). More importantly, an electronic version of the document was also publically posted on Google Documents so others could easily dissiminate the manifesto-like document without having to come into

---

[4] http://www.facebook.com/media/set/?set=a.133967863308873.12078.133634216675571&type=1
[5] See translation in Annex D. Original version can be found here:
http://www.facebook.com/note.php?note_id=197190613628100&comments

physical possession of the document (see Appendix D). These "rules of engagement" were thus relatively easy to distribute online to both Egyptian and international audiences.

Because the protest page attracted so many followers, it also became a place for other likeminded political parties, such as the April 6 Youth Movement to share links to their Facebook page and events (see Appendix A, Fig. 14). While the Khaled page's January 25 event was the main event for the online protest movement, several offshoots of the protest were created that were catered to specific neighborhoods. Despite the variety of January 25 events, both the Khaled and April 6 Youth Movement pages linked to the same public Google document where the mission, strategy, and tactics were located.

Facebook also became a hub where Egyptians could share visual media like photos and videos in real time (see Fig. 3). Some of these items were also cross-linked to Twitter and YouTube, making them compatible across the social media spectrum. On the English version of the Khaled page, graphic photos were posted on July 20, 2010 that drew international attention and increased awareness of both the Arabic and English versions of the protest pages (Emon, Lust and Macklin 2011). There, the public could discuss the photos and their grievances with the government without physically exposing themselves to danger. Facebook user Alzahrae Elmasry said on July 21, 2010,

> *Please we need to gather all photos and videos exposing police brutality,*
>
> *assaults and violation of any human rights. This file must be as*
>
> *adocumentation and evidences that should be presented to the highest*
>
> *juridical authority in Egypt with all the names of the victims themselves*
>
> *and the parents of the victims and the witnesses, they can shut up dozen*

cases by lies and terrorism but they cannot silence thousand cases against

them (Emon, Lust and Macklin 2011).

Facebook users also used the platform to circulate photos of neutral military

behavior and to underline public support for them. Leil Zahra Mortada, a female

Fig. 4 Photos from both amateur photographers and mainstream media of positive interaction between civilians and authorities were shared easily and at no cost during the revolution (Facebook).

activist posted a photo on January 28, 2011 that depicted an older woman kissing a

neutral riot policeman (see Fig. 4). On the same post, user Redhuan D. Oon wrote,

"Subhanallah! How can you soldier shoot your own mother?"

Serving as a virtual satellite truck for the masses, social media allowed videos to

be uploaded and viewed worldwide easily with few barriers. Facebook was used to

spread amateur video during the lead up to January 25 and thereafter. On January 18,

2011, activist Asmaa Mahfouz made a plea on YouTube that was also embedded in the

Khaled page where she called on Egyptians to support the January 25 protest event organized by the Khaled page that was also hosting her video (see Fig. 5). One of many postings of the same Mahfouz's video attracted over 2,700 "likes" and more than 82,000 people subscribed to her updates on Facebook. Because of this exposure on the social web, Mahfouz was able to attract the attention of the international mainstream media, like the *New York Times*, who wrote a feature story about her on February 1, 2011 (El-Naggar 2011).

When all of Facebook's capabilities were used together with other social media, the amplification effects could be great. Ushahidi co-founder and Fletcher School PhD Patrick Meier noted in his iRevolution blog that Egyptians were actively sharing tactical knowledge on Facebook with almost military-like organization. As protesters gained more experience encountering police, they were able to take lessons learned, compile them into electronic manuals, share them in hardcopy and online, and then constantly improve methods by offering feedback on social media sites (see Fig. 6) (Meier 2011). Meier notes that some of the manuals used Google Earth imagery and

Fig. 5 Activist Mahfouz declares her support for the January 25 protests at Tahrir Square (ElShaheed 2011).

stressed the importance of nonviolent engagement with police and the military. In all of these examples, Facebook allowed for the instant and virtually free distribution of this knowledge to those with an Internet connection (Meier 2011).

The "We are all Khaled Said" Facebook page continues to be an important hub for Egyptian political discussion and played an important role in the June 2, 2012 return of thousands of protesters to Tahrir Square to demand justice in the Mubarak trial. The page created another protest event on Facebook attracting more than 155,741 accepted

invitations to the June 7, 2012 march. Just as during the January 25, 2011 call to protest, a link to a manifesto hosted on Google Documents was included with a list of peaceful demands, suggesting Facebook activism in Egypt will remain relevant (El Shaheed 2012).

Fig. 6 Example of a sketch explaining how to gather without being detected and then surge into main streets to overwhelm opposition forces (Meier 2011).

5.3. YouTube and the January 25 Revolution

Cellphone videos posted on YouTube have played an important role in spreading protest videos rapidly within Egypt and beyond. Indeed, in June 2010, an Egyptian cellphone user uploaded morgue photos of the badly disfigured Khaled Said that were turned into martyr videos on YouTube and gained millions of views ("Meet Asmaa Mahfouz" 2011).

Fig. 7 Video memorializing Khaled Said with more than 264,279 views. Scenes also show acts of nonviolent protest, police brutality, and children holding signs reading "We are all Khaled Said." ("Our People's Uprising" 2011)

While there is an established history of martyrdom videos being produced in the Middle East glamorizing armed fighters, martyr videos portraying nonviolent actors began to emerge in Egyptian nonviolent struggle. The image of a smiling Said were displayed next to images of his badly disfigured face with music and slogans like "we are all Khaled Said," according to Egyptian activist Ahmed Zidan (El-Naggar 2011). The images quickly spread beyond Egypt and into the newsrooms of major outlets like Al-Jazeera, The New York Times, and CNN. The photos and videos inspired Google executive Wael Gholim to secretly establish the "We are all Said Khaled" Facebook page, which attracted more than 180,000 followers when it first began in June 2010. That

25

page would later be the platform specifically used to call for the January 25, 2011 protests that led to the collapse of the Mubarak regime (El-Naggar 2011).

On the day of the January 25, 2011 protests, the New York Times catalogued and commented on several amateur videos as they became available on YouTube. The first video to be featured was a cell phone video posted by YouTube user "lukasjakubika" that showed a crowd of civilians peacefully marching towards Tahrir Square in broad daylight with some holding signs. The video had over 700,000 views by May 28, 2011. Another video posted by user "MrPeopleNews" showed a large crowd of young men peacefully holding banners, chanting slogans, and flashing red cards as they made their way to Tahrir. More than 40 other clips were posted by "MrPeopleNews," and news agencies like Al Jazeera began broadcasting his videos and attributing images to him. On February 5, 2011, Al Jazeera blogged, "We've said it before: Egyptians from all walks of life, young and old, have joined the protests. MrPeopleNews posted this video yesterday of a five-year-old leading the chants" (see Fig. 8).

Fig. 8 Al Jazeera features an amateur video of a young boy leading protest chants in Egypt (Al Jazeera 2011).

In another example of amateur video going viral and reaching the mainstream media, user "TheKingTut86" showed a police vehicle in Cairo careening through the streets indiscriminately into a crowd of nonviolent protesters, colliding with at least one bystander and continuing on. The footage was picked up by Al-Jazeera and then broadcast around the world. The footage was used by newsrooms to highlight the regime's disorder and its disregard for human life (Jardin 2011).

Videos were not just used to document and highlight violence, but also used as a call to action. Egyptian activist Asmaa Mahfouz used YouTube on January 18, 2011 to call on protesters not to simply "follow" the "We are all Said Khaled" Facebook protest page, but to gather in person on January 25, 2011 and to bring family members along with them. If each person brought 5 or 10 others with them, she said, they might possibly force out the Hosni Mubarak regime. One version of the amateur video has been viewed more than 509,295 times and gained the attention of *The New York Times* on February 1, 2011, which wrote a full feature on her. There she was quoted as saying she does not only rely only on Facebook and Twitter, but also speaking to people face to face. That is how she films herself in the YouTube video, with her face towards the audience. Despite her slight dismissal of social media's importance in revolution, it may be reasonable to assert that she herself would not have reached *The New York Times* and a broader international audience had it not been for her YouTube video.

Indeed, there are literally thousands of examples of YouTube videos of the revolution that were uploaded and attracted hundreds of thousands of views. A Google search of keywords "Tahrir Square Egypt" in English alone on YouTube results in around 16,600 videos as of May 23, 2012. As in the examples mentioned above, the mainstream media, once the sole source for international video reporting, is using more footage taken from ordinary individuals, making each activist a potential international reporter.

Twitter and the January 25 Revolution

Since its use in the 2009 Green Revolution in Iran, the demand for Twitter as a social media platform for dissidents in the Middle East has grown in importance, as noted by Assistant Secretary of State for Public Affairs P.J. Crowley (Landler and Stetler 2009). In the Iranian example, it was deemed important enough to antiauthoritarian demonstrators there that U.S. Secretary of State Hillary Clinton's staff asked Twitter not to perform scheduled maintenance that could interrupt the flow of information between Iranians and the outside world (Landler and Stetler 2009). In Egypt's January 25 Revolution, Twitter was again heavily used by nonviolent struggle groups.

Twitter allows for massive volumes of small texts to be created and distributed, making organization of the texts a challenge. One of the important organization and social features of Twitter use in Egypt was the "hashtag"[6] #Jan25, along with others like #Egypt and #Tahrir, according to journalist Catharine Smith (2011), Egyptian activist Dalia Ziada, and many others.

Twitter hashtags allowed those using the microblogging application to post categorized information to the Internet in real time using computers, cellphones, smartphones, and voice-to-tweets over telephone. As in the Iranian Green Revolution of

---

[6] A *hashtag* is a keyword with a pound sign (#) that Twitter users can use to associate their tweet with an ad-hoc conversation stream. Anyone can add a hashtag to their tweets and thus have their tweets enter the conversation stream for that particular topic. Hashtags may be planned ahead of time, spontaneously, or intuitively. For instance, #OBL became the spontaneous hashtag for tweets about the death of Osama Bin Laden in May 2011.

2009, Egyptian Twitter users in Egypt using hashtags were able to share intelligence in

real time in order to coordinate movements and identify ad-hoc medical aid stations,

according to Cairo Reuters producer Maryam Ishani (2011). The Egyptian Front to

Defend Protesters (EDFP), according to Ishani, was able to use Twitter "to pass

important emergency numbers, locate detained demonstrators, and dispatch legal aid,"

frustrating government efforts to silence opposition.

In an interview for Twitter's Hope140 blog, the Egyptian activist (username

alya1989262) credited with first using the #Jan25 hashtag, explained the importance of

Twitter for her movement:

> *Twitter is a very important tool for protesters, as evidenced by*
>
> *the fact it and Facebook were repeatedly blocked in Egypt as*
>
> *the protests flared up. We use it to campaign and spread the*
>
> *word about protests/stands–hashtags are invaluable in that*
>
> *respect, and to share news quickly and efficiently, with our own*
>
> *140-char commentary on them, and subsequently have*
>
> *conversations with random people/complete strangers. But*
>
> *most importantly, it allows us to share on the ground info like*
>
> *police brutality, things to watch out for, activists getting*
>
> *arrested, etc.* (hope140.org 2011).

Activist Dalia Ziada's use of social media to promote nonviolent struggle both leading up to the January 25 revolution and continuing to this day has centered around strategic messaging, virtual pamphleteering, and information sharing with likeminded activists. Throughout the 2011 Egyptian Revolution, Ziada messaged several times daily (more than 36,000 tweets to date) to her more than 25,000 Twitter followers on themes such as social justice, nonviolent struggle, and tolerance (@daliaziada 2011).

As an influential blogger and Twitter user, the tweets she created and those she retweeted reached a wider audience than may have been possible through traditional media, which was under state control. Ziada used Twitter on several occasions, as did others, to promote nonviolent resistance and confront those who suggested that force should be used.

Fig. 9 Twitter user shares a nonviolent tactic with other protesters (@alya1989262 2011).

In response to a suggestion from someone that force should be met by force, Ziada tweeted: "Shame on you, Esam Sharaf! "@AleyOsama: @daliaziada #tahrir yes he said so, that we are against violence but we will use it when we have to" (@daliaziada 2011).

Whereas underground printing presses were needed to distribute Solidarity's messages in communist Poland in the 1980s, Ziada and others were able to use the Internet to distribute her message around Egypt and the world with fewer physical logistical challenges. In another example that caught the attention of the *Washington Post* (Cavna 2011), Ziada tweeted links to electronic copies of an educational comic book in

Arabic describing nonviolent struggle in Martin Luther King, Jr.'s Montgomery Bus Boycott (Hamsa 2008). During the revolution, she tweeted, "Dalia Ziada: Can a comic book about Martin Luther King change the Middle East? http://daliaziada.blogspot.com/2009/05/can-co … #Egypt #Tunisia #Algeria #Yemen." (@daliaziada 2011) Both Twitter and Facebook provided Ziada with more platforms through which she could share her blog writings and other nonviolent struggle materials with a wider audience.

Twitter as a platform to quickly disseminate lessons learned and tactics in real time was demonstrated repeatedly during the revolution. Demonstrators shared tips on how to mitigate the effects of tear gas, how to stop police vehicles nonviolently, and where arrests were being made. Tweets with the code "RT" means that the tweet is being copied and tweeted again, or retweeted. In an example of this kind of use, username *fahmy_shahin* tweeted that protesters should let the air out of police vehicle tires, a tip that was picked up and retweeted across Twitter by users like the influential user *alya1989262*, creating a ripple effect (see Fig. 8) (@alya1989262 2011).

Twitter was also used as a platform to share information about the location of pro-Mubarak elements. Not only was the international media able to use this independent information to monitor events in Egypt, but protestors were able to maintain awareness and maneuver to avoid contact with hostile elements. In one example of many, Ziada retweets a photo tweet posted by username *Salamander* showing pro-Mubarak elements "heading towards tahrir from adbel moneim riyad sq downtown…"(@daliaziada 2011). Twitter appeared useful in documenting evidence of weapons used against protesters, too. User, *gahdasha*, reposted Twitter photos that her daughter, username *nazlyhussein*, took and posted on the Internet of expended ammunition reportedly used on peaceful protestors. The photo depicts metal canisters with "70 Meter Short Range Projectile" clearly written in English on the side. A shotgun shell of unknown origin is also shown in the picture. Twitter user, *MtwfiQ*, posted an amateur photo that was viewed more than 4,000 times of a tear gas canister with "Made in the USA" clearly visible on it. Soon after, major news networks used the exact same photos, with ABC News's Christiane Amanpour on January 28, 2011 commenting, "the tweets and the social media posts are coming in in huge blasts, expressing disappointment with the United States, which is not good at this precise moment" (Shami and Wali 2011). In an ABC interview about the teargas canisters, Egyptian Aly Eltayeb said, "the way I see it the U.S. administration supports dictators" (see Fig. 9) (Shami and Wali 2011). The report and discussion was sparked by the amateur Twitter photo, whereas in the past, this story may have not been reported, or may have only been reported had a professional journalist been on site.

Finally, Twitter was used to call crowds to protest, provide them assurance that the protest was underway in observably large numbers, and share news about how the authorities were reacting to the protests. On January 15, 2011, Twitter user *Alyouka* reposted the popular online activist *alya1989262*'s tweet

Fig. 10 Twitter user shares an image of a projectile with "Made in the USA" on it, gains attention of international press (inset)

"http://on.fb.me/fBoJWT over 16000 of us are taking to the streets on #jan25! join us: http://on.fb.me/fQosDi #egypt #tunisia #revolution" (@alya1989262 2011). Deciphered, this tweet provides links to a Facebook event page where people can express their intent to attend a mass protest, provides the number of protesters committed to date, and includes hashtags to ensure the message is categorized for ease of reference by those following #Jan25, for instance. This example also displays the interconnectedness of Twitter and Facebook in coordinating action.

Twitter users shared photos of masses marching towards Tahrir Square on January 25 as well. In one example, Twitter user *Gsquare86* posts a photo of dozens men making their way to Tahrir early in the day, suggesting that the protest was actually occurring and there was security in numbers. These images were retweeted to others and also picked up by the international press (@gsquare86 2011) Popular Twitter user *Sandmonkey* tweeted, "Huge demo going to tahrir (liberation square, downtown) #jan25 shit just got real." Although short and colloquial, his tweet was retweeted across cyberspace and consumed by Egyptians and international media alike. Mainstream media like PBS, who reported that they had been following *Sandmonkey*'s tweets for years, tracked him down in February 2011 and interviewed Mahmoud Salem in person (Glinsky 2011).

Twitter became a tool for sharing the official reaction to protests on January 25 as well. Twitter user *Zeinabo* tweeted, "Protesters shaking hands of police officers after they let them thru, thousands headed to kasr el nil #jan25" (@alya1989262 2011). This post was retweeted by Twitter user *Alyouka* and her more than 2,000 followers and many other users retweeted to their users, creating a ripple effect and helping others with access to this information gauge what areas were permissive.

RT @Salamander Pro mubarak protesters heading towards tahrir from abdel moneim riyad sq downtown #Egypt #Jan25 http://twitpic.com/3vqmjo

Fig. 11 Twitter user posts photos of pro-Mubarak demonstrators along with their location (@daliaziada 2011).

Internet connectivity in Egypt during the revolution

In an example of how mass action can weaken a dictator in unexpected ways, and an example that proved especially well suited to social media, Egyptian authorities faced a classic dictator's dilemma when it decided to cut off Internet access. It was unable to censor the tsunami of unfiltered information, but shutting down Internet service providers and cell phone service could also harm the Egyptian economy (Kalathil and Boas 2003). On January 28 the Egyptian authorities ordered 90% of all Internet and mobile providers to suspend their services, according to Matt Richtel (2011) of the *New York Times*. By cutting off virtually all of the country from the Internet and mobile phone service, merchants and apolitical actors alike became disenfranchised with the Mubarak regime, only adding to the growing number of citizens growing politicized and angrier with the government. Indeed, Richtel (2011) says that Queens University of Charlotte professor and Egyptian Mohammed el-Nawawy said that those who would have simply vented their anger on Facebook or blogs then took to the streets once their "safe" outlet was denied them. Mubarak's censorship appeared to create the exact opposite effect he was seeking to create. In fact, the Facebook page credited with organizing the January 25 protest grew to over 1,000,000 members immediately following the ban reversal.[7]

With even more people representing a broader spectrum of Egyptians taking to the streets, Mubarak's regime resorted to violence. This included jets over Tahrir Square, regime supporters with clubs and razor attacking protesters, and raiders on camel and horseback charging through crowds of nonviolent protestors (Ritchel 2011). This further aggravated ordinary citizens and coincided with a spike in violent activity on both sides. Seeking to deescalate the violence, precipitated by extreme censorship, Mubarak restored mobile phone and Internet access on February 2, but also began attempting to hack into Facebook and Twitter accounts to gain personal identity information and map dissident networks (Abell 2011).

Al-Jazeera, Facebook, Twitter, and YouTube became alternatives to official state media and traditional outlets still tightly controlled by the government. According to Dina Zayed, the Egyptian state media had "more than a dozen terrestrial and satellite channels, at least as many radio stations and some two dozen state newspapers and magazines"(Zayed 2011). Much of their efforts centered around a strategic communications theme that the protesters were controlled by Hamas or other foreign entities, or simply protesting for free food (Zayed 2011). However, social media allowed Egyptians to bypass the state media and even mock it, parading with signs in Tahrir Square while eating hamburgers. Those who were not connected directly to social media were able to hear about developments through social connections that were either directly or indirectly connected to a social media source, according to Egyptian human rights activist Dalia Ziada (Ziada Interview 2011).

---

[7] The "We are all Khaled Said" Facebook page had 1,503,879 members as of July 17, 2011.

6. Analysis

As mentioned in the *Methodology* section, this paper seeks to apply Sharp and Ackerman's theories on nonviolent struggle to observations about social media use in the 2011 Egyptian Revolution and determine if there is a relationship between the technology and nonviolent conflict principles in action. The hypotheses and indicators are detailed below with supporting observations.

Social media was used in the 2011 Egyptian Revolution to promote unity of movement. Through primary (Egyptian blogs and an in-person interview) and secondary sources (media reports), the author holds that there is significant evidence of social media being used to promote unity of movement in the January 25 Revolution. In the examples provided in the case study, which is only a snapshot of thousands of like examples Indicator 1a, *social media was used to publicize agendas*, was reasonably present.

In the example of the "We are all Khaled Said" Facebook page, in both Arabic and English, it clearly established its agenda in very specific terms. When it created the January 25, 2011 Police Day protest event invite on Facebook, the event details included links to the Google Document nonviolence manifesto and included a code of conduct and specific demands of the government on the event description page. That page attracted more than 90,000 people (Fig. 2) and resulted in similar event pages being created by entities such as the April 6 Youth Movement (Appendix A, Fig. 14). This also reflects nonviolent weapons 3 *Declarations by organizations and institutions* and 180 *Alternative communications* because social media does not fit into the tradition media categories outlined in 9-12 of Appendix E, 198 Nonviolent Weapons.

Egyptians also used YouTube to bypass mainstream media and promote their agendas. In Asmaa Mahfouz's YouTube example, she used the platform on January 16, 2011 to call on Egyptians to support the upcoming protest and the "We are all Khaled Said" Facebook page. One version of the video was seen over half a million times. Her video appeal was also shared on Facebook and Twitter (Fig. 5). Nonviolent weapons 122 *Literature and speeches advocating resistance* and 180 *Alternative communication* may apply in this case. 1 *Public speeches* and 63 *Social disobedience* may apply if one considers online activity a "public" act. This author holds that is a reasonable assertion, but that is beyond the research scope of this paper.

Twitter was used by Egyptians to spread the link to the "We are all Khaled Said" January 25 protest page and Google document containing the movement's agenda in detail: demands, rules of engagement, and legal defense information. For example, Twitter user *Alyouka* retweeted calls by *alya1989262* on January 15, 2011 to click on the link for the event where the agenda was hosted (see page 35).

Indicator 1b, *social media was used to call people to action*, in addition to being present in the above examples, each example also demonstrates how the protest agenda was collocated with the protest event information. Specific examples of call to action include Asmaa Mahfouz's January 18, 2011 video calling Egyptians to protest on January 25 and to bring at least 5 other people with them. This video was linked on the "We are all Khaled Said" Facebook page (Fig. 5) and as a standalone video on YouTube. The Facebook video included a link to the January 25 protest with the specific time and location of the event, along with a link to the agenda already mentioned (Appendix A, Fig. 13). As mentioned above, one example of this video (there are many) was seen more than 500,000 times and attracted mainstream media like *The New York Times* (see page 27).

Calls to action were also sparked by Facebook photomontages of police brutality (Fig. 3) that inspired anger in protestors. One may observe Facebook user Alzahrae Elmasry's post who called on Egyptians to post photos and video of brutality on the Internet in order to expose corruption (see page 23). In this example, a call to action by a photomontage author creates a ripple effect inspiring others to reinforce the call to action and make their own declarations and post photos.

In an example similar to the agenda criteria that demonstrates this ripple effect, *Alyouka* was one of many who retweeted calls by *alya1989262*, on January 15, 2011 to join in protest on January 25 and included links to the protest Facebook event page, where the agenda, location, and schedule for the protest was kept.

The Indicator 1c, *social media was used to spread propaganda*, is present in the many examples provided in the case study, such as when activist Dalia Ziada used Twitter links and her blog to distribute e-comic books of Martin Luther King, Jr.'s Montgomery Bus Boycott story, an effort Western media reported on (page 33). Apart from simply using social media as a distribution channel, it is important to note the convenience and relatively lower risk factors associated with electronic distribution versus that of print materials. This appears to be an advantage that social media offers in some cases.

Propaganda in the form of martyr images have become a commonplace in the January 25 Revolution, in art, video, and photography. Figure 7 highlights a YouTube video that shows patriotic and national images mixed to music and Khaled Said's portrait. Also included in the video are images of protesters peacefully defying a protest ban. The version of the video referenced in this paper was seen more than 200,000 times and contains promotional links to the "We are all Khaled Said" Facebook page, the same page that called for the January 25, 2011 protest.

In another example of propaganda, Twitter username *MtwfiQ*, posted a Twitter photo of ammunition reportedly used on peaceful protestors (Fig. 10). The gas canisters clearly had "Made in the USA" on them, which drew the attention of the international media and sparked critical conversations about American support for Mubarak. This contributed to a "name and shame" campaign to usurp Mubarak's foreign support bases.

Propaganda highlighting the role of women in the revolution was also a feature of nonviolent struggle social media. Protesters posted photos of Egyptian women confronting authority (in some cases being beaten). Leil Zahra Mortada, a female activist, posted a photo on January 28, 2011 that depicted an older woman kissing a neutral riot policeman (Fig. 5). It was one of 181 photos she complied and shared on Facebook that were subsequently shared by others. While the "kiss" photo may be viewed as a novelty, both the act and its promotion have very specific roots in nonviolent struggle technique, and may be considered 33 *Fraternization* and 136 *Disguised disobedience.*

In another example, the January 18, 2011 Asmaa Mahfouz YouTube video was used by the administrators of the "We are all Khaled Said" Facebook (which also invokes heroic art, see Appendix A, Fig. 12) page to gain publicity for their January 25 protest while at the same time calling for young men to protect the honor of female protesters. Despite the threat of secret police and Mubarak's government still being in power, 2,741 people liked the video calling for revolution (Fig. 6).

In each of the propaganda examples described above, the charactaristics of many nonviolent weapons are present, most notably those in the category of "communications with a wider audience" and "social intervention."

Social media was used as a planning tool

The author holds that there is substantial evidence both within this paper and on the broader public record that social media was not only a broadcast media tool, but also a planning tool. As mentioned in this paper, the Egyptian Front to Defend Protesters (EDFP) was able to report the location of political prisoners and Twitter users were able to report on the columns of police forces and pro-Mubarak groups moving through the city, supporting Indicator 2a, *social media was used to collect field intelligence.* With such intelligence, the EDFP, "We are all Khaled Said" Facebook page followers, and many other individual actors were able to plan their movements towards Tahrir Square to minimize contact with hostile forces. This behavior was also present in the Green Revolution in Tehran, Iran in 2009 (Shapiro 2009).

Indicator 2a may also be observed in how the "We are all Khaled Said" Facebook and Twitter page was used to share information about police movements on specific streets (page 36). This meets Sharp's political defiance criteria for being widely dispersed but also concentrated on a specific objective. For instance, social media could be used to share photos, or call all members to a specific location while providing updates on police locations in real time.

Twitter was heavily used to gather information from the field and share it. In one typical example, Appendix C, Fig. 18 shows a tweet by Dalia Ziada she retweeted from *Salamander* with a photo and street address of pro-Mubarak supporters moving towards protesters "heading towards tahrir from adbel moneim riyad sq downtown…"

(@daliaziada 2011).

In another typical example, Twitter user Zainabo tweeted that police were shaking the hands of protesters and letting them pass without problems near Kasr el Nil, which signaled a safe passage in that moment (page 36). This was then retweeted to other Twitter users with the #Jan25 hashtag. This is an act of political defiance as defined by Sharp because it is aggravating a weakness of the dictatorship and can sever its sources of power. Publicizing incidents of policemen refusing to beat protesters and women kissing soldiers as if to reward them for good behavior may undermine the violence demanded of the dictator.

Undermining the image of superiority while also providing actionable data that other protesters may use to plan a permissive approach to Tahrir Square was a task Twitter was well suited for. Twitter user *Gsquare86* accomplished two tasks with one tweet (see Appendix C, Fig. 20) of reporting that police were "everywhere" and had cordoned off Shubra (threat report) with that of posting a photo clearly showing a large group of protesters making their way to the city center (reinforcement report). Her tweets were retweeted and followed by other protesters.

YouTube proved to be a highly visible source of information on protest element maneuver. User *lukasjakubika* posted a YouTube video on January 25 from his building window of a very large group of protestors moving along a major street in Cairo with signs and flags (Annex B, Fig. 15) and footage of the police trailing them timidly. This footage was used by international media and other protesters to guage the resolve of the police and strength of the protest movement.

Indicator 2b, *social media was used to coordinate maneuver*, is indirectly evident in the examples provided in Indicator 2a, and there were thousands of tweets declaring where protesters should rally to best avoid hazards in real time. However, the best explicit example that can be verified by the author is a Google document (see Annex D) that clearly sets out January 25 rally points in specific neighborhoods and maneuver strategies, with telephone numbers. For example, the document explains for the protest in the city of Ismailia (Suez): "Thalathini Street and Railroad Street next to Hamzawy - call link on Facebook in Ismailia." In this example, the general location is given, with instructions to refer to Facebook for the exact times and details. For Alexandria, two specific rally points are identified (see Fig. D) for a time of 9 a.m. with instructions to "talk [take] back alleyways." In all, the document provides at least seven rally point instructions.

While the Google document provided the master plan, or manifesto, Facebook and Twitter were tools used to distribute the maneuver instructions (see Appendix A, Fig. 13 and 14, and p. 36). A social link shortening program called Bit.ly was also used to generate the link to the document, http://bit.ly/Egypt25 (Annex A, Fig. 13). Bit.ly users can track user statistics with the program. Because of the wide dissimination, this meets Sharp's political defiance critera as it is difficult for the regime to combat, especially when considering the dictator's dillema blocking the Internet presented. When the regime did try to cut the internet, it created a public backlash and negaitve economic consequences.

Indicator 2c, *social media was used to share operational knowledge and lessons learned*, is evident in several examples, such as when Twitter user *fahmy_shahin* tweeted that protesters should let the air out of police vehicle tires to render them immobile

(Fig. 9). This information was retweeted and shared across the Internet once it was posted. Patrick Meier highlighted examples of Egyptian April 6th Movement leader Ahmed Salah using tactics gained from an anonymous nonviolent struggle e-book. Salah tweets to his follower about remaining in back alleys before surging into main streets, and provides this guidance in real time (Fig. 6) with the warning that social media was being monitored by authorities (Meier 2011).

Sharing lessons learned when probing for the best approach to Tahrir, Twitter user *Zainabo* informed the public of a permissive environment near Kasr el Nil where police were shaking the hands of protesters and letting them pass (Fig. 21). This was then retweeted to other Twitter users with the #Jan25 hashtag who could exploit the weakness and reach their objective. In this example, knowledge was crowdsourced spontaneously.

In an example of a more deliberate and organized use of social media to manage operational information, the Egyptian Front to Defend Protesters (EDFP), according to a member, was able to use Twitter "to pass important emergency numbers, locate detained demonstrators, and dispatch legal aid," frustrating government efforts to silence opposition (Meier 2011, 31). Prominent Twitter user *alya1989262*, who was featured in an interview with the Twitter official blog, said "*it allows us to share on the ground info like police brutality, things to watch out for, activists getting arrested, etc.*"(Meier2011).

Social media was used to promote nonviolent discipline

Nonviolent struggle is a constant theme in communications related to the January 25 Revolution and social media associated with it. A strong example of Indicator 3a, *codes of nonviolent conduct and values are embedded in communications*, may be observed clearly in the January 25 protest agenda hosted on Google Documents (Appendix D) that served as a de facto manifesto with its 20 political parties and well-known individuals signing their names to it. Parties included the Muslim Brotherhood and April 6th Youth Movement, and individuals included Said's mother and Mohammed El Baradei. The document was shared on the "We are all Khaled Said" Facebook page and Twitter (Appendix A, Fig. 13-14) and included the messages:

> *...the demonstration...peaceful. We are advocates of peace and we*
> *are not advocates of violence. We demand our rights, and the first*
> *to preserve the rights of others. Will not respond to any attempts to*
> *provoke the security... show restraint and not recklessness and to*
> *do anything against the law or endangering the lives of any person*
> *to cause danger or damage to any property, public or private*[8]

In this example, the manifesto clearly prohibits violence while at the same time overtly commiting to public order.

In an example of public, individual appeals to nonviolent discipline, in the January 18, 2011 YouTube video of Asmaa Mahfouz calling for Egyptians to support the January 25 protest scheduled on the "We are all Khaled Said" Facebook page, she says:

> *We demand our basic human rights...instead of catching ourselves*
> *on fire, let us do something positive and gather on January 25...if*
> *each person brings five or ten people with them, we can make a*
> *difference...tell your friends, post it on the Internet, send it by SMS*
> *or Facebook...(Meet Asmaa Mafouz 2011)*

Mahfouz's alluding to a self-immolation case in Tunisia as something other than "positive" is interesting. Indeed, self-immolation is not listed as one of the 198 weapons of nonviolence. She uses social media to announce her disapproval of martyrdom in favor of nonviolent weapons 38 *marches,* 47 *assemblies of protest or support,* 15 *group*

---

[8] Basic Google translation of the Annex D January 25 Protest document.

lobbying, 122 *literature and speeches advocating resistance,* and other methods outlined by Sharp. This popular video reinforces the values outlined in the manifesto and calls on others to follow the spirit of that guidance as well.

The nonviolence imperative runs throughout the overall January 25 movement's messages. Examples of Indicator 3b, *the public openly publicizes their own acts of nonviolence,* include Leil Zahra Mortada, a female Egyptian activist, posted a photo on January 28, 2011 that depicted an older woman kissing a neutral riot policeman (see Fig. 4). On the same post, user Redhuan D. Oon wrote, "Subhanallah! How can you soldier shoot your own mother?" The photo was part of a larger photomontage of Egyptian women protesting nonviolently.

In another example of promoting the movement's own nonviolent behavior and its potential rewards, and as highlighted above, Twitter user *Zainabo* tweeted that police were shaking the hands of protesters and letting them pass without problems near Kasr el Nil, which helped highlight the peaceful nature of the protesters and some police (Fig. 21). Reinforcing the image of the protester as victim and not lawbreaker, the "We are all Khaled Said" Facebook page posted and hosted thousands of photos of peaceful demonstrators. In one particular example (Fig. 3), photos were posted of Egyptians standing five feet apart and facing the sea as individuals, exploiting a loophole in the protest laws, seeming to illustrate the power of peaceful protest to overwhelm the government's ability to respond to each act, conforming to 173 *nonviolent occupation,* 193 *overloading of administrative systems,* 196 *civil disobedience of "neutral" laws,* and others.

In an example of YouTube being used to publicize the movement's own nonviolence, a video tribute to Khaled Said (Fig. 7) was one of many that featured scenes of protesters peacefully defying security forces and contrasted it with scenes of police brutality. The video culminates with a series of children and women holding signs that read "We are all Khaled Said" in Arabic. Indeed, none of the media linked to the Google Documents manifesto and the January 25 protest displayed acts of violence, although reports of violence did exist between some protesters and government forces. This suggests not only discipline of message, but a strong commitment to disciplined nonviolent struggle even when faced with physical violence.

The January 25 protest movement was disciplined in denouncing violence, even in situations where violence in self-defense may be tempting. This discipline was essential to maintaining the nonviolent character of the movement and thus avoids the slippery slope of violent resistance. Examples of Indicator 3c, *violent instigators are confronted, shunned publically*, include the January 25 protest guidance posted on Google Documents, shared across social media as mentioned above, specifically states:

> *Must show restraint and not recklessness and to do anything*
> *against the law or endangering the lives of any person to cause*
> *danger or damage to any property, public or private. In the case of*
> *the presence of any members of any violent act Baiqoumoua please*
> *bloc about the person and ruled out an immediate protest from*
> *within and to inform the security about it.*[9]

In another example, when the first post revolutionary prime minister Esam Sharaf was accused of saying violence was justified against protesters if necessary by Twitter user *AleyOsama* to Dalia Ziada, she responded via Twitter, "Shame on you, Esam Sharaf!..." (see Fig.32). Ziada has more than 25,000 Twitter followers. Both examples above also fits Sharp's political defiance charactaristic of not accepting the outcome will be accepted

---

[9] Basic Google translation of the Annex D of January 25 Protest document.

by the means of fighting chosen by the dictator. By avoiding violence, protestors attack the dictator's weakness, not his strength.

Sharp's mass action conditions

Sharp argues that a key to undermining dictatorships is to create mass action to create four conditions. Based on the examples outlined above, the author will briefly test each of these four conditions below.

The oppressed population themselves in their determination, self-confidence, and resistance skills are strengthened

Social media was used as a platform for self-expression, encouragement, and knowledge sharing. In the examples of Mahfouz's YouTube video call to protest, the "We are all Khaled Said" Facebook events page, and Twitter tactics sharing, the author holds it is reasonable believe the oppressed who were connected to the Internet and also turned their virtual activism into real life action chose to do so because they felt strengthened by social media.

Independent social groups and institutions of oppressed people are created

As sociologist Philip N. Howard (2011) states, "digital media are social networks" that shouldn't be discounted because they are not face-to-face. The author holds that social media, like the Facebook page "We are all Khaled Said," are a form of independent social groups. Other online political entities, such as the April 6 Youth Movement may be considered independent institutions.

A powerful internal resistance force is created

The author holds that it is reasonable to believe social media emboldened internal resistance by giving its users more information in which to determine their level of risk

47

and advantage (whether to protest, what roads to take, which authorities were less likely to take punitive measures). While social media in and of itself may not be a powerful internal resistance force, when used as a tool by nonviolent struggle actors, it may magnify the organizational capacity and responsiveness of the organization, which may translate into greater power.

A wise grand strategic plan for liberation and implement it skillfully is developed

Links to the January 25 protest manifesto hosted on Google Documents was a common feature among a diverse range of opposition media (see Appendix D). The manifesto clearly espoused nonviolent principles, contained a clear plan of action, listed its demands, and was undersigned by at least seven prominent Egyptian activists and NGOs. While this may not have directly led to Mubarak's downfall, the January 25 protest was clearly instigated by an online call to action, specifically linked to a Facebook event created on the Kahlid Said page, which consequently led to Mubarak's defeat.

7. Conclusions and Recommendations

According to the preceding research, initial indications suggest that social media appears to have amplified nonviolent struggle in the January 25, 2011 Revolution. The examples of social media used in the case studies were representative of literally hundreds, if not thousands, of similar content that surged across the web. The examples provided demonstrate that many Egyptians were able to break state information monopolies to communicate not only to other Egyptians, but the international community as well. Additionally, collaboration between Egyptians using social media – sharing content, setting dates for rallies, creating propaganda – suggest that online media became a form of alternative social structure. Perhaps it was this new structure that allowed people to build the confidence and momentum needed to create effective mass nonviolent struggle on January 25, 2011.

But giving social media credit for creating a revolution is much like giving a hammer credit for building a house. As this paper attempts to illustrate, social media can be a highly effective tool when implemented as part of a strategy, a blueprint. As this paper has described, Sharp and Ackerman's theories were connected directly to the successful Otpor movement in Serbia that would become Canvas, a pro-democracy NGO. Canvas and the International Center for Nonviolent Conflict then influenced and mentored Egyptian activists in organizing their own nonviolent struggle. Those skills would be applied by the undersigners of the Google Documents January 25 Manifesto in creating a strategy of nonviolent struggle using social media as a tool. Based on this paper's analysis and case studies, social media appears to be highly efficient in consolidating many of the 198 nonviolent weapons capabilities into a potent tool of unprecedented usefulness, a nonviolent struggle "force multiplier."

However, this is not a capability exclusive to nonviolent movements. Indeed, social media may be used to commit crimes such as the 2011 London Riots or organize extremist groups. Nonviolent struggle social media and violent social media may not be mutually exclusive, as they are mere tools. The intent behind the use of tools, if it is informed by strategy, may have an increased probability of success if social media offers a comparative advantage over other tools available.

As this paper discusses, the "We are all Kahlid Said" Facebook page was the exclusive platform on which the January 25 protest was first publicized with a link to the Google Documents Manifesto. While the Facebook event certainly announced the January 25, 2011 protest date first and attracted enough attention to act as a catalyst for broad public support for the protest and the tipping point it created, it did so as part of a concerted effort, a preconceived plan that deliberately pursued a strategy of nonviolent struggle. As this paper seeks to illustrate, the core cause of the January 25, 2011 protest was the coordinated implementation of a strategy of nonviolent struggle, with the effect being the successful implementation of tactics, which included using social media, not vice versa. So in this sense, and when considering the examples provided in this paper, social media does appear provide a powerful tool in facilitating nonviolent struggle.

The use of social media in creating positive change in society is welcome to many, but there are also consequences that may not yet be fully understood. When Alfred Nobel invented TNT, he intended to create a new material that would improve development, moving tons of rock in a single blast. Little did he know that his technology would be added to the list of others that have dual uses in both peace and violence. In some ways, social media is the digital TNT of the 21st century. It is inherently dynamic and can be used for good or evil.

Optimism about online activism in support of nonviolent struggle may be tempered by the fact that just as citizens have adapted social media to their needs, governments and other actors are quickly learning how to adapt to the volatile social media operations environment. There are several dangers online activists may face that are growing in complexity. For instance, government agents may pose as activists online and infiltrate networks and gain access to information about a contact's friends and family. Opponents may also flood social media with misinformation, setting traps for activists, such as proposing false meeting points for a rally or medical aid stations during violent events. In Tunisia, the government was able to successfully compromise thousands of Facebook accounts in an effort to target dissidents (Goodin 2011).

While social media as a command and control tool, a force multiplier in military terms, has inherent dual use potential, democratic governments such as the United States may seek to promote the nonviolent use of information technology to strengthen social discourse. Countries like the U.S. may also consider placing restrictions on the export of information technology services and goods that may be used to oppress nonviolent movements. This may include security consulting by American private security firms, banning the export of surveillance infrastructure and censorship software like "Websense," software employed to filter out pornography and other unwanted sites at public internet access points and workplaces in the U.S., but often used to block political sites and block access to outside news (Manev 2011). As sentiment analysis and predictive analytics become more sophisticated outside of traditional intelligence and defense organizations and hit the public market, this may also endanger online democracy-building efforts. Export of this knowledge may also be banned for export to larger, more stable countries such as Russia and China, who may "weaponize" censorship resources imported from the West and then repackage them for export to less stable countries, such as Iran. Additionally, the U.S. State Department, Department of Defense, and NGOs interested in liberal democracy should study how strategic social media may influence nonviolent movements, develop best practices in not only disseminating the technology, but how to use it effectively, and help spread that knowledge to other nonviolent movements. In the realm of defense, this assistance may prove more effective in some cases than armed conflict.

To be sure, the ultimate political outcome of the 2011 Egyptian Revolution remains ambiguous, but the fact that the nonviolent movement there was able to bring down a regime with a popular, indigenous effort is largely accepted. To some thought leaders, social media was the driving force behind the nonviolent overthrow of the Mubarak regime. To others, social media is a passing fad that had little or no role in the success of the nonviolent revolution there. The author submits that these arguments, often framed in the absolutism of tech utopianism or rejectionism, will require thorough study and data collection in focus groups and surveys to map what exactly influenced ordinary individuals to put themselves at risk on January 25, 2011. On-site interviewing and polling of Egyptians would be helpful to determine to what degree those protesting on Egypt's streets were encouraged to do so by social media or by someone with access to it. The author believes that social media was an important tool in enhancing nonviolent struggle strategy so that it could reach critical mass, or tipping point, and attract popular support. While debate about the role of social media in the Egyptian Revolution will certainly continue, it is difficult to imagine the January 25, 2011 revolution in Egypt occurring successfully without a sound strategy of nonviolent struggle employing social media as one of its main tactics.

8. Bibliography

Abdulla, Rasha A. "Taking the E-Train: The Development of the Internet in Egypt." *Global Media and Communication* 1, no. 2 (2005): 149-165

Abell, John C. 'Egypt internet restored; Cairo protests turn violent". *Wired* http://www.wired.com/epicenter/2011/02/egypt-internet-back-up-as-protests-turn-violent-in-cairo/ (accessed July 17, 2011).

Ackerman, Peter. Key elements of civil resistance. YouTube video, 4:36, Posted by "Nonviolent Conflict". Febuary 1, 2012.http://www.youtube.com/watch?v=yYXPlkCffcI. (accessed July 17, 2011).

Ackerman, Peter. and Jack Duvall. *A force more powerful.* New York: Palgrave, 2000.

Ackerman, Spencer. 2007. U.S. has secret tools to force internet on dictators. http://www.wired.com/dangerroom/2011/02/secret-tools-force-net/. (accessed July 17, 2011).

Al Jazeera. "Live Blog Feb. 5 – Egypt Protests." Febuary 5, 2011 http://blogs.aljazeera.com/blog/middle-east/live-blog-feb-5-egypt-protests

Al Jazeera. "Q&A: Gene Sharp: Al Jazeera talks with the quiet but influential scholar of non-violent struggle." December 6, 2011. http://www.aljazeera.com/indepth/opinion/2011/12/201112113179492201.html

"المنصورة :يوم الغضب على التعذيب والفقر والفساد والبطالة"(Almansoura: Day of Rage for Torture, Poverty, Corruption and Unemployment). *Facebook.* https://www.facebook.com/events/190222594337244/

Anonymous. 2011. ElShaneed. *Facebook.* http://www.facebook.com/ElShaheeed. (accessed July 17, 2011).

Arab American National Museum. Panel Discussion: Revolution + Social Media. *iTunes Podcast.* http://www.arabamericanmuseum.org/revolution.social.media.panel. (accessed July 17, 2011).

Ari Mel. Malcolm Gladwell Surfaces to Knock Social Media in Egypt. *The Nation.* http://www.thenation.com/blog/158241/malcolm-gladwell-surfaces-knock-social-media-egypt. (accessed July 17, 2011).

@alya1989262.Twitter Profile.*Twitter.* https://twitter.com/alya1989262/status/29956738308378624

Ayyad, Khayrat. "The Use of the Internet by NGOs to Promote Government Accountability: The Case of Egypt." In *African Media and the Digital Public Sphere,* edited by Okoth Fred Mudhai, Wisdom J. Tettey, and Fackson Banda, 89-104. New York: Palgrave MacMillan, 2009.

Bard, Mirna. 15 Categories of Social Media. *Mirna Bard.* http://www.mirnabard.com/wp-content/uploads/2010/02/TheSocialWeb1.jpg. (accessed July 17, 2011).

Basic concepts. *International Center for Nonviolent Conflict.* http://www.nonviolent-conflict.org/index.php/what-is-icnc/icnc-basic-concepts. (accessed July 17, 2011).

Beirut. Social Media Utilized to Organize Protests in Egypt. *Thought Pick.* http://blog.thoughtpick.com/2011/01/social-media-utilized-to-organize-protests-in-egypt.html. (accessed July 17, 2011).

Bradley, Matt "Egyptian Protest Leader to Take Break From Google, Form Tech NGO." *Wall Street Journal..* April 24, 2011. http://online.wsj.com/article/SB10001424052748704123204576283340694707516.html

Burkhart, Grey E. and Susan Older. *The Information Revolution in the Middle East and North Africa.* Washington, DC: Rand, 2003.

Castells, Manuel. *Communication Power.* Oxford: Oxford University Press, 2009.

Cavna , Michael. "Amid Revolution, Arab Cartoonists are Drawing Attention." *Washington Post.* Sunday, March 6, 2011. http://www.washingtonpost.com/wp-dyn/content/article/2011/03/06/AR2011030602980.html

Chadwick, Andrew, and Philip N. Howard, eds. *Handbook of Internet Politics.* London: Routledge, 2009.

CNN. "Egypt Uprising: Hosni Mubarak Steps Down; Interview With Wael Ghonim: The Egyptian People Are the Leaders and Heroes of This Revolution." http://transcripts.cnn.com/TRANSCRIPTS/1102/11/bn.02.html. (accessed May 16 2012).

Diebert, Ronald. "The Geopolitics of Internet Control." In *Routledge Handbook of International Politics,* edited by Andrew Chadwick and Philip N. Howard. London: Routledge, 2008.

El-Neggar, Mona. "Equal Rights Takes to the Barricades." *New York Times.* Febuary 1, 2011. http://www.nytimes.com/2011/02/02/world/middleeast/02iht-letter02.html

Emon, Anver M., Ellen Lust, and Audrey Macklin."We Are All Khaled Said: An Interview with the Administrators of the Facebook Page that Fueled the Egyptian Revolution." *Boston Review.* November 3, 2011. http://www.bostonreview.net/BR36.6/khaled_said_facebook_egypt_revolution.php

Fattah, Alaa Abd El. "In Egypt, YouTube Trumps Facebook." In *PostGlobal: Need to Know.* Washington, DC: The Washington Post/Newsweek, 2008.

Frequently Asked Questions. *International Center for Nonviolent Conflict.* http://www.nonviolent-conflict.org/index.php/what-is-icnc/icnc-frequently-asked-questions. (accessed July 17, 2011).

@gdasha.*Yfrog.com.* 2011 http://yfrog.com/hsviyjlj

Ghareeb, Edmund. "New Media and the Information Revolution in the Arab World: An Assessment." *Middle East Journal* 54, no. 3 (2000): 395-418.

Giglio, Mike. "ElShaheed: The Mysterious "Anonymous" Behind Egypt's Revolt." *Newsweek.* January 03, 2011. http://www.newsweek.com/2011/01/30/el-shaheed-the-mysterious-anonymous-behind-egypt-s-revolt.html. (accessed July 17, 2011).

Gilinsky, Jaron." Egyptian 'Sandmonkey' Blogger Unmasks Himself in Cairo." *PBS.* February 14, 2011. http://www.pbs.org/mediashift/2011/02/egyptian-sandmonkey-blogger-unmasks-himself-in-cairo045.html

Gladwell, Malcom. "Small Change: Why the revolution will not be tweeted.*" New Yorker*, October 4, 2010.. http://www.newyorker.com/ (accessed October 3, 2010)

Glanz, James. U.S. Underwrites Internet Detour Around Censors Abroad - NYTimes.com. *New York Times.* http://www.nytimes.com/2011/06/12/world/12internet.html?pagewanted=all. (accessed July 17, 2011).

Globe and Mail. "How a Brutal Beating and Facebook Led to Egyptian Protests." http://www.theglobeandmail.com/news/world/africa-mideast/how-a-brutal-beating-and-%20facebook-led-to-egyptian-protests/article1884156/page1/

Goodin, Dan. Tunisia plants country-wide keystroke logger on Facebook. *The Register.* http://www.theregister.co.uk/2011/01/25/tunisia_facebook_password_slurping/.(accessed July 17, 2011).

@gsquare86. *Yfrog.com.* 2011. http://yfrog.com/h8fvzvrj

Hamsa. Martin Luther King and the Montgomery Story (Arabic). http://issuu.com/hamsa/docs/mlk/2. (accessed July 17, 2011).

Howard, Phillip N. *The digital origins of dictatorship and democracy: information technology and political Islam.* Oxford University Press, 2010.

Howard, Phillip N. "The Arab Spring's Cascading Effects." *Pacific Standard* . February 23, 2011. http://www.psmag.com/politics/the-cascading-effects-of-the-arab-spring-28575/

Ishani, Maryam. Foreign Policy: Scramble To Silence Cairo Protests. *National Public Radio.* http://www.npr.org/2011/01/28/133306415/foreign-policy-scramble-to-silence-cairo-protests. (accessed July 17, 2011).

James, J. "Bridging the Digital Divide with Low-Cost Information Technologies." *Journal of information Science* 27, no. 4 (2001): 211-217.

Jardin, Xeni. Egypt: Al Jazeera video shows police running over protesters. *Boingboing.net*. http://www.boingboing.net/2011/02/03/egypt-al-jazeera-vid.html. (accessed July 17, 2011).

Kalathil, Shanthi, and Taylor C. Boas. *Open Networks, Closed Regimes: The Impact of the Internet on Authoritarian Rule*. Washington, DC: Carnegie Endowment for International Peace, 2003.

Khalaf, Roula. "US non-violence centre trained Egypt activists." *Financial Times*. http://www.ft.com/intl/cms/s/0/73dd11a4-38e3-11e0-b0f6-00144feabdc0.html#axzz1RERK3Lck. (accessed July 17, 2011).

Landler, Mark and Brian Stetler. "Washington Taps Into a Potent New Force in Diplomacy." *New York Times*. June, 16 2009

Mahfouz Asmaa. "Meet Asmaa Mahfouz and the Vlog that Helped Spark the Revolution" YouTube video, 4:36, Posted by "iyadelbaghdadi". Febuary 1, 2011.

Maney, Kevin. 2011. U.S. technology has been used to block, censor Net for years. *USA Today*. http://www.usatoday.com/money/industries/technology/maney/2006-02-21-net-censor_x.htm. (accessed July 17, 2011). "

Meier, Patrick. Civil Resistance Tactics Used in Egypt's Revolution #Jan25 | iRevolution. *iRevolution*. http://irevolution.net/2011/02/27/tactics-egypt-revolution-jan25/.(accessed July 17, 2011).

Michaeal, Dunn. "New Media, New Politics? From Satellite Television to the Internet in the Arab World / New Media in the Muslim World: The Emerging Public Sphere / Arabizing the Internet." *The Middle East Journal* 54, no. 3 (2000): 465.

Michaels, Jim. 2011. Tech-savvy youths led the way in Egypt protests. *USA Today*. http://www.usatoday.com/news/world/2011-02-07-egyptyouth07_ST_N.htm. (accessed July 17, 2011).

@MtwfiQ .2011. *Yfrog.com* http://yfrog.com/h0uh3dbj

"إهداء إلى الشهيد خالد سعيد   شعبنا قامت قيامته"(Our People's Uprising: Dedicated to the Matyr Khaled Said) YouTube video, 4:38 Posted by "TheShaheeed." Febuary 1, 2012

PC Magazine Encyclopedia. "Definition of Youtube" http://www.pcmag.com/encyclopedia_term/0,1237,t=YouTube&i=57119,00.asp

PC Magazine Encyclopedia. "Definition of Twitter" http://www.pcmag.com/encyclopedia_term/0%2C1237%2Ct%3DTwitter&i%3D57880%2C00.asp

Pellegrino, Greg. 2008. Managing Digital Exhaust: How New Technologies Are Leading a Revolution in Government Decision Making. *Deloitte Dbriefs Webcast.* http://www.deloitte.com/view/en_US/us/Insights/Browse-by-Content-Type/dbriefs-webcasts/0859ab21df9be210VgnVCM1000001a56f00aRCRD.htm?id=sm_ps.reporting/2010/10/04/101004fa_fact_gladwell?currentPage=all (accessed July 17, 2011).

"Protest in Egypt" YouTube video, 3:58 Posted by "lukasjakubicka" January 25, 2012 http://www.youtube.com/watch?v=GcLmi0ZdEpc

Richtel, Matt. Egypt Cuts Off Most Internet and Cellphone Service. *New York Times.* http://www.nytimes.com/2011/01/29/technology/internet/29cutoff.html. (accessed July 17, 2011).

Rugh, William. *Arab Mass Media: Newspapers, Radio, and Television in Arab Politics.* Westport, CT: Praeger, 2004.

Shapiro, Samantha M. "Revolution, Facebook-Style." *New York Times Magazine,* January 22, 2009.

Sharp, Gene. "Open letter from Gene Sharp to Thierry Meyssan." *Voltairenet.org* http://www.voltairenet.org/The-Albert-Einstein-Institution (accessed July 17, 2011).

Sharp, Gene. *From dictatorship to democracy.* London: Serpent's Tail, 2011.

Sharp, Gene. *Waging nonviolent struggle.* Boston: Extending Horizons Books, 2007.

Shirky, Clay. "The Political Power of Social Media". *Foreign Affairs.* January/February 2011 http://www.foreignaffairs.com/articles/67038/clay-shirky/the-political-power-of-social-media. (accessed July 17, 2011).

Shortell, Timothy. "What is power?" http://www.shortell.org/courses/cs3/power.html. (accessed July 17, 2011).

Smith, Catharine. "Egyptian Tweeter, First To Use "#Jan25," Says Twitter Was "Invaluable" During Protests". http://www.huffingtonpost.com/2011/02/17/egypt-twitter-jan25-protests_n_824310.html. (accessed July 17, 2011).

Socialbakers." Egypt Facebook Statistics. http://www.socialbakers.com/facebook-statistics/egypt"

Social media - Definition. *Merriam Webster Dictionary Online.* http://www.merriam-webster.com/dictionary/social+media?show=0&t=1310852028. (accessed July 17, 2011).

Stolberg, Sheryl G. "Shy U.S. Intellectual Created Playbook Used in a Revolution." *New York Times.* February 16, 2011. http://www.nytimes.com/2011/02/17/world/middleeast/17sharp.html?_r=2&pagewanted=all

Wali, Sarah O. and Deena A. Sami. "Egyptian Police Using U.S.-Made Tear Gas Against Demonstrators."*ABC News.* January 28, 2011 http://abcnews.go.com/Blotter/egypt-protest-police-us-made-tear-gas-demonstrators/story?id=12785598#.T8nODr82WMl

What Is It? *International Center for Nonviolent Conflict.* http://www.nonviolent-conflict.org/index.php/what-is-icnc. (accessed July 17, 2011).

Wheeler, Deborah L. "Working Around the State: Internet Use and Political Identity in the Arab World." In *The Handbook of Internet Politics*, edited by Andrew Chadwick and Philip N. Howard. London: Routledge, 2008.

Zayed, Dina. Egypt state media run to catch up with revolution. http://www.reuters.com/article/2011/02/11/us-egypt-media-coverage-idUSTRE71A3LT20110211. (accessed July 17, 2011).

Ziada, Dalia. 2011. @Daliaziada on Twitter. *Twitter.* http://twitter.com/#!/daliaziada. (accessed July 17, 2011).

Ziada, Dalia. July 14 2011. Personal Interview.

APPENDICES

Appendix A: Egyptian Facebook screen captures

This appendix features figures created from screen captures of actual Facebook pages.

Fig. 12 "We are all Khaled Said Facebook page with photos, events, notes, and other information (El Shaheeed 2011).

Fig. 13 "We are all Khaled Said" January 25˙ protest guidance and links to Google Document. This served as a kind of manifesto (El Shaheeed 2011).

Fig. 14 Facebook page for the April 6 Youth Movement, which displays an event highlighting the January 25, 2011 protest. More than 2,000 people from one neighborhood committed to attend despite it being illegal ("Day of Rage" 2011).

Appendix B: Egyptian YouTube screen captures

This appendix features figures created from screen captures of actual YouTube pages.

Fig. 15 Video taken by tourist of protesters moving towards Tahrir Square on January 25, 2011 that was later broadcast by mainstream news outlets (Protest in Egypt 2011).

C: Egyptian Twitter Screen Captures

This appendix features figures created from screen captures of actual Twitter pages.

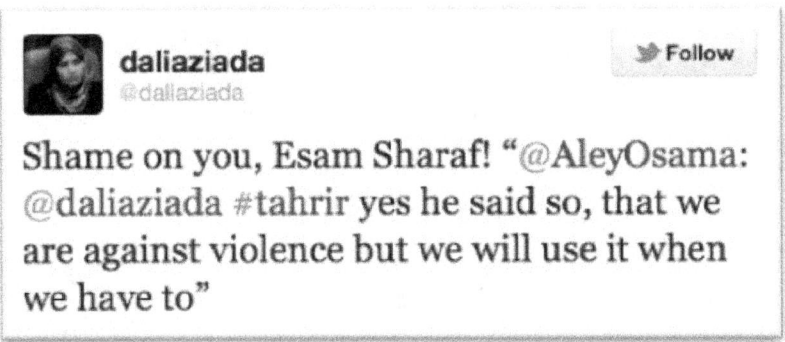

Fig. 16 Activist Dalia Ziada responds to a suggestion that violence could be used by the opposition (Ziada 2011).

Fig. 17 Influential activist Alyouka provides a link as early as January 15 to the January 25 protest manifesto and link to the Facebook event at "We are all Khaled Said." (@alya1989262 2011)

Fig. 18 Twitter photo including location information of hostile pro-Mubarak crown moving along a road (Ziada 2010).

Fig. 19 Twitter photo of ammunition being shared between two users. This photo was retweeted and available to anyone searching Arabic key words (@ghdasha 2011).

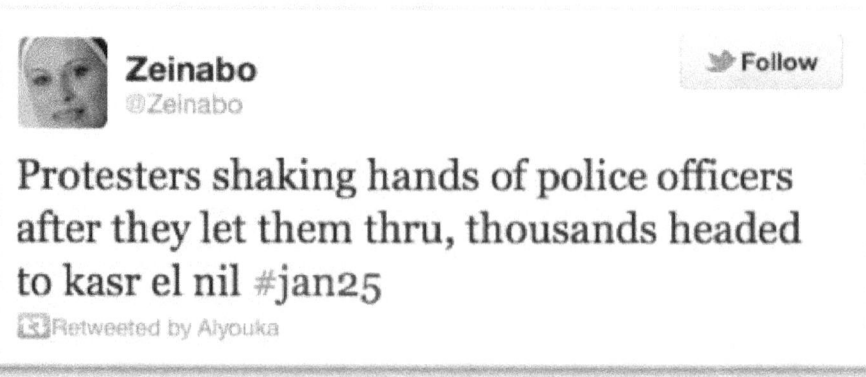

Gsquare86 1 year 4 months ago

People joining ..but square is cordoned and police every where #jan25 shubra

yfrog.com/h8fvzvrj

Reply   Tweet   Favorite

Fig. 20 Twitter photo posted by protester and retweeted by others. Gives the viewer an impression of the crowd while warning about police. Photo also uses hashtag #Jan25 (@gsquare86 2011).

Zeinabo
@Zeinabo

Follow

Protesters shaking hands of police officers after they let them thru, thousands headed to kasr el nil #jan25

Retweeted by Alyouka

Fig. 21 Twitter post reporting on police behavior at "kasr el nil" (@alya1989262 2011).

Appendix D: January 25 Protest Declaration on Google Documents

This appendix features figures the original Arabic document declaring the January 25, 2011 protests on Police Day and a Google Translate version of the document below it.

http://bit.ly/Egypt25

كل ما تريد أن تعرفه عن مظاهرات ثورة يوم 25

نحن من
لماذا نتظاهر؟
لماذا يوم 25 يناير؟
ما هي مطالبنا؟
أماكن وتوقيت المظاهرات
إرشادات للتظاهر
مهمة تليفونات
لينكات تهمك
المظاهرة في يشاركون

ملاحظة هامة: يرجى زيارة الصفحة بشكل مستمر حيث أنه سيتم تحديثها بكل جديد
نحن من
عشان اتعملت الفيسبوك على صفحة وهي سعيد خالد كلنا صفحة من يناير 25 يوم للتظاهر بدأت الدعوة
الدعوة 2010. يونيو إسكندرية في الشارع في والضرب التعذيب من اتقتل اللي سعيد خالد الشهيد قضية
تونس وبسبب الدعوة نشرت ما وبعد. يشعب أو سياسية قوى أي من لها مخططا يكن ولم عفوية كانت
أو حركة أو جماعة أو حزب أي تتبع لا الصفحة. الفكرة ونشر بالمشاركة للمطالبة المصريين كل تشجع
عن الدفاع يريدون الذين المصريين لكل هي فكرة أو شخصا تؤيد لا وهي بذاتها مستقلة فالصفحة جمعية
نجاحها سر كان وده الصفحة في الأعضاء من اتيةذ جود على قائمة والصفحة. حقوقهم
لماذا نتظاهر؟
المصرية الحكومة تذكرها التي التقارير فبرغم. النواحي كل في التاريخية مراحلها أسوأ من بواحدة مصر تمر
،للنهاية بداية هو 25 يوم جميعا ونزلونا. التقارير تلك عن مختلفة الحقيقية وللأسف أنه إلا الصورة لتجميل
والمطالبة الإيجابية من جديدة لصفحة وبداية بالدنا في يحدث لما والخنوع والرضا الصمت كل نهاية
الاهتمام بدأنا أننا لها لننقول الحكومة ضد ثورة هو لكن إنقلاب بمعنى ثورة مش هو يناير 25 يوم. بالحقوق
اليوم بعد نسكت ولن حقوقنا لكل وسنأخذ البعض بعضنا بشؤون

ألف مائة من وأكثر الجسمي مرضى ونص مليون منهم بالالكتئاب مريض مصري مليون 30 فهناك
ونصف مليونان منهم فقير مليون 48 لدينا. شخص 5000 وفاة في تسببت 2009 عام خلال انتحار محاولة
في نيعيشو ونصف مليون ومنهم مأوى أي بدون مصري مليون 12 لدينا. مدقع فقر في يعيشون المليون
المقابر.

فقط واحد عام خلال جنيه مليار 39 من بأكثر جميعا قيمتها تزيد فساد قضايا وجود إلى أدى منهجي فساد هناك
تحتل ومصر. الحكومي الفساد حيث من العالمين التنافسية تقرير في دولة 139 بين 115 المركز

بين الأخير المركز تحتل ومصر 30% تجاوزت شبابالبين البطالة ونسبة عاطل شاب مليون 3 من أكثر هناك
التوظيف في الشفافية معدل في دولة 139

تقريبا مصر أطفال ونصف. ولادة 1000 كل طفل خمسين بواقع العالم في الأطفال لوفيات معدل أعلى لدينا
سنويا رطانبالبالس مصاب ألف 100 من أكثر ولدينا. سي بفيروس مصاب شخص مليين 8 بأنيميا مصابون
مواطن ألف 35 لكل إسعاف سيارة ولديتا. المياه تلوث بسبب.

وجود دون منهم الآلاف على والقبض التعذيب من المصريين عشرات وفاة في تسبب للطوارئ قانون مصر في
فقد نشاطهم وإجهاض السياسيين لمراقبة الأمن استخدام وبسبب. عليهم القبض لعمليات قانوني سند أي
من أكثر على يحصل الحاكم الحزب أن إلى أدى الشعب مجلس انتخابات في فاضح تزوير ذلك عن نتج
المجلس مقاعد من بالمائة تسعين.

الفيديو هذا مشاهدة يرجى المعلومات هذه ومصادر المزيد لمعرفة.
لماذا يوم 25 يناير؟
فاستشهد وجيوشه بدباباته البريطاني الجيش العادية الشرطة بهندقهم جهاز في أجدادنا قاوم 1952 عام في
سنة خمسين من أكثر بعد ونحن. الوطن أجل من التضحية في الأمثلة أروع وضربوا 100 من أكثر وأسر 50 منهم

67

بالذات اليوم هذا اخترنا وقد .وإهانتهم المصريين لتعذيب أداة أصبح الذي جهاز الشرطة ممارسات من الآن نعاني
لأن المحترمون الضباط معنا يلتحم أن المظاهرة يوم نرجو ما وهذا الشعب مع الشرطة التحام إلى يرمز لأنه
.أعمالهم دون تعطيل لمشاركة المصريين لكل يمنح مما رسميا إجازة هو يناير 25 يوم .واحدة قضيتنا
مطالبنا؟ هي ما

الأدنى الحد بزيادة المصري القضاء حكم باحترام وذلك تنفجر أن قبل الفقر مشكلة مواجهة :**المطلب الأول**
صرف على والعمل .للشعب المقدمة للخدمات لتحسين والتعليم الصحة مجالات في خاصة عادلة زيادة للأجور
لفترة وذلك وظيفة على الحصول يستطيع لا جامعي خريج شاب لكل مصري جنيه 500 إلى تصل إعانات
.محددة

على والقبض مصر على الأمني الجهاز سيطرة في تسببت والتي الطوارئ حالة إلغاء :**المطلب الثاني**
على النيابة سيطرة بفرض نطالب ونحن .ذنب أي دون المعتقلات في وضعهم الحكومة لسياسات المعارضين
القضاء أحكاما وتنفيذ .الشرطة أقسام في ممارستها يتم التي المنهجية التعذيب عمليات لوقف سامالأق
.المصرية الحكومة قبل من واحترامها

في متمثل مصر تواجه الذي الأمني الانفلات بسبب العادلي حبيب الداخلية وزير إقالة :**المطلب الثالث**
الرادع وجود دون الداخلية وزارة من عناصر أو ضباط يد على حدثت يالت الجرائم وانتشار الإرهابية الحوادث
.القوي

ولأنه مفسدة المطلقة السلطة لأن متمثالتيتين فترترتين تتجاوز لا بحيث الرئاسة مدة تحديد :**المطلب الرابع**
ئيسنار نختار أن حقنا من .منصبه في السنين عشرات البقاء الجمهورية لرئيس تسمح متقدمة دولة توجد لا
.يموت حتى البلاد في فيحكم بالسلطة أحد يستبد ألا حقنا ومن

بعض مع نتحرك إننا هي والبداية والتعليم الصحة زي مجالات في المصريين لكل كثيرة مطالب هناك طبعا
أداءها على ونحاسبها الحكومة نوجه إننا كشعب دورنا وده الحكومة على الضغط طريق عن مطلب ونحقق
.العكس مش أولوياتها ونحدد
المظاهرات وتوقيت أماكن

حال عن نتحرك إننا هي والبداية ومش ومظلومة متضايقة كلها الناس .معانا الناس كل نحشد إننا هو المظاهرة هدف إن نفهم إننا جدا مهم
تنزل والناس الشعبية المناطق لكل في مسيرات نعمل عايزين لكده و عشان يشاركوا نشجعهم لازم البلد يبقى
مش للمظاهرات أماكن فكرة و على .جدا مهم ده المظاهرة مكان لحد أشخاص عشر أكثر من سيرات في بعض مع
في مظاهرات فيها وهيتنظم عنها يعلن لم تانية أماكن في مظاهرات فيه لأن هنا من المذكورة الأماكن على مقصورة
.العلي تقدر اللي بالطريقة و غضبك رأيك عن وتعبر تنزل إنك المهم .مختلفة محافظات

الكبرى القاهرة
شبرا دوران
المطرية دوران
القاهرة جامعة أمام
العربية الدول جامعة شارع

لو وحلوان والجيزة القاهرة أنحاء كل في شعبية أحياء في ومسيرات مظاهرات منظمة جهات أخرى فيه :مهمة ملاحظات
.ليهم وانضم يناير 25 يوم شعبية منطقة في كنت

الإسكندرية
تتحرك أن على .المنشرية ميدان هو الثاني والمكان مصر محطة ميدان هو الأول المكان :للوقفة مكانين تحديد مت
نقاط إلى لا للوصول وذلك الجانبية الشوارع أو الكورنيش عبر تسير الاسكندرية مناطق كل من كل من مسيرات
.بالضبط المظاهرة توقيت في التجمع

صباحا 9 بعد الثالث يوم اتصلوا التفاصيل ولمعرفة عنها معلن غير ماكنأ من ستخرج أخرى مظاهرات فيه
0151543978 :التليفون على

الإسماعيلية
يلي الإسماعي في الفيسبوك على الدعوة رابط - حمزاوي بجوار الحديد السكة وشارع الثلاثيني شارع

المنصورة
في الفيسبوك على الدعوة رابط متابعة وللمعلومات يناير 24 الموافق الاتنين يوم المكان تحديد سيتم
المنصورة

الفيوم
.ظهرا الثانية الساعة تمام الفيوم ببندر الحواتم ميدان من تبدأ الفيوم أهالي بها سيقوم كبيرة مسيرة

68

المحلة الكبرى

في الإعلان عنه سيتم خامس مكان في التجمع وسيتم والجمهورية الشعبية ومنطقة الشون وميدان البندر ميدان المظاهرة. رابط الدعوة

طنطا

بالضبط الثانية الساعة والتجمع طنطا بمدينة المحافظة مبنى أمام

سوهاج

في الفيسبوك على الدعوة رابط متابعة وللمعلومات يناير 24 الموافق الاتنين يوم المكان تحديد سيتم سوهاج

منسقي أرقام على للحصول تهمك أرقام لفقرة والوصول الصفحة لأسفل للنزول يرجى :الأماكن باقي
محافظتك في المظاهرات.
التظاهر إرشادات

الآخرين حقوق على نحافظ أن الأولى ومن بحقوقنا نطالب نحن. عنف دعاة ولسنا سلام دعاة نحن .سلمية المظاهرة هدف. ليه بيخططوا هما اللي ويحصل شعورنا نم يخرجنا عشان الأمن من استفزاز محاولات لأي نستجيب لن ضبط يجب .البلد يخربوا عايزين بلطجية شوية إنهم على المتظاهرين تصويرو هو الأمن أهداف من رئيسي بأي الإضرار في يتسبب أو لخطر شخص أي حياة أو يعرض أو القانون يخالف شيء أي عمل والتدهور وعدم النفس الشخص حول التكتل يرجى عنيف عمل بأي بيقوموا أفراد أي تواجد حالة وفي .خاصة أو عامة ممتلكات عنه الأمن وإبلاغ المظاهرة داخل من الفوري واستبعاده.

واحتمال الجهود تشتتيت في يتسبب التأخير .بالدقيقة الدقيقة المحدد الوقت في المظاهرة مكان في التواجد يرجى منعها .فرصة الأمن على ويصعب المظاهرة دأب السهل من يجعل الوقت نفس في التواجد .المظاهرة فشل

بطاقتك احمل .البنوك بطاقات أو الرخص أو كارنيهات مثل تحتاجه لا شيء أي تحمل لا البيت من النزول عند الأفضل الزي .بسهولة تتكسر حاجة أي ساعتك متجيبش ريت ويا .طوارئ لأي كافي ومبلغ الشخصية طويل لوقت الاعتصام أم المظاهرة استمرار حالة في البرد من للحمامية كيتة وجود مع جينز أو رياضي يكون المياه في عجز في دايما بيكون المظاهرة داخل لأنه كبيرة مياه قزازة معاه يجيب شخص كل ريت يا.

يرجى إحضار علم مصر وعدم إحضار أي شعارات أو لافتات خاصة بأي حزب أو حركة أو جماعة أو جمعية أو فئة يرجى عايزين ومش الاجتماعية والعدالة الحقوق في بالمساواة جميعا نطالب لأننا المصريين لكل اليوم .دينية نتفرق.

على خبرة أكثر هم لمن الأمامية الصفوف واترك الأمامية الصفوف في تكن لا مظاهرات لأي نزولك عدم حالة في القرارات تخاذا في لخبطة محيصلش عشان المسيرة أو المظاهرة قيادة.

الأمن أفراد مع جانبية معارك في الدخول أو بذيئة ألفاظ أي استخدام عدم يرجى .عليها ومتفق موحدة الهتافات طاعته عدم حالة وفي الدور بهذا القيام على الجيش في خدمته أثناء إجباره تم مجند هو .هو عدوك هو مش المركزي الأمن الحقيقي عدوك عدو نحو غضبك مشاعر تركز الإمكان بقدر حاول .باتالعقو بأقصى معاقبته يتم للأوامر.

طبعا .بحقوقنا نطالب نحن المواطنين نعاقب لا نحن. الشوارع في المرور تعطيلي لعدم الإمكان قدر المحاولة المرور تعطيلي سيتم شوارع أي في الآلاف عشرات نزول حالة في لأنه .للمرور المتعمد التعطيلي عن باتكلم علي. كلم اللي هد ده ومش بنتكلم.

حد مع تكون ريت يا دي الظروف في بيفيدوا الأصحاب لأن لوحدك متنزلش جدا مهم أكرر .. لوحدك متنزلش المظاهرات وقت الاستادات بننزل ما زي .بعض مع تتنزلوا صاحبك حد واقنع.

الموحدة الهتافات

واحدة إيد ونكون صفوفنا نوحد ولازم لمصر بننزل كلنا .التظاهر أفكار أهم من هي الموحدة الهتافات فكرة بتهم اللي القضايا دي لأن والفقر البطالة قضايا على ونركز كلنا بعض مع بالهتافات هنلتزم علي: الاتفاق تم اللي الهتافات ودي كلهم، المصريين

مصر تحيا .. مصر تحيا
إنسانية لكرامة .. حرية .. عيش
حرية .. حرية .. حرية
وبينك بيننا الطوارئ .. فينك فينك حرية يا
الواطي الصوت كرهنا إحنا .. هنطاطي مش هنخاف مش

هتغيب مش الثورة شمس .. حبيبي يا تونس شعب
وطن أي يا نفديك .. بالدم بالروح
خلاص الظلم كرهنا احنا .. للناس قول صوتك ارفع
المصريين احنا .. اتنين واحد
هتهون مش بلدنا مصر .. الكون وهز الخلق صحي
والمدام اللص هرب .. قام تونس شعب لما
يثور كله ما الشعب قبل .. للأجور أدنى حد
بتكفيش ما والملاليم .. وأعيش شغل ألاقي حقي
مفتوح باب الحرية .. الروح صحي مصري يا يلا
تشوف تصحى الدنيا خلي .. الخوف هَي شعب يا يللا
الدين ليوم طاطيهي مش .. سنين ومجد حضارة شعب
مهمة تليفونات
المحاميين مع التواصل
على والحفاظ المتظاهرين دعم في المتخصصين المحاميين من مجموعة وهم مصر متظاهري الدفاع عن جبهة أرقام
حقوقهم:
0120624003 - 0129295510 - 0106701470

المظاهرات منسقي مع التواصل
الكبرى القاهرة: 0105805657 & 0123077912 & 01521543977 & 0102864919
الإسكندرية: 01521543978
الدقهلية: 01521543976 & 0172320006
أسوان: 01521543979
الغربية: 01521543982 & 0187606131
الإسماعيلية: 01521543984 & 0103977677
بورسعيد: 01521921386 & 0104496590
أسيوط: 0144373186
سوهاج: 0177740064 & 0187627090
بني سويف: 01521543983
السويس: 01521921385
الأحمر البحر: 01512934066
القليوبية: 01521921380
الشرقية: 01521543981
قنا والأقصر: 01521543980
لينكات لهمك
الإنترنت على سعيد خالد كلنا صفحة
والتعذيب والظلم والبطالة الفساد على الثورة ليوم للدعوة الرئيسية الصفحة
المظاهرات في المشاركين لحماية مصر محاميين بوقفة الخاصة الدعوة
مصر متظاهري الدفاع عن جبهة

المظاهرات في يشاركون
بالسياسة المهتمة غير المصرية الجماهير من ستكون المظاهرات هذه في الأكبر المشاركة أن إلى الإشارة يجب.
صفحة من وخرجت مسيسة غير خرجت الأساس من الدعوة فإن ولهذا. ومأسيهم مشاكلهم ولمست وصلتهم الدعوة لأن
القوى جميع للدعوة استجابت وقد. سياسي هدف ذات حركات أو أحزاب أي تتبع لا والتي "سعيد خالد كلنا"
المصريين حقوق عن للدفاع بالأساس قامت السياسية القوى هذه ولأن واحدة المطالب لأن السياسية.
أبريل 6 شباب حركة
التغيير مطالب لدعم الشعبية الحملة
الغد حزب
والحرية العدالة أجل من شباب
لمسلمين الإخوان جماعة
الوفد حزب
حشد حركة
الديموقراطية الجبهة حزب
التغيير مطالب لدعم البرادعي رابطة
الكرامة حزب
صباحي حمدين دعم حملة
الثوريون الاشتراكيون
البلتاجي محمد الدكتور
الأسواني علاء الأستاذ

70

AWAY WITH THE GATEKEEPERS

سعيد خالد يدالشهه والدة
فضل بلال الساخر الكاتب
الخضضيري محمود المستشار
والكد عمرو الفنان
دياب محمد المخرج
النجا أبو خالد الفنان

Translation of above document from Google Translate

If the following link Mstgch read it from here

Who We Are

Began to call for demonstrations on 25 January of the page are all Khaled Said a page on Facebook Ashan work was the issue of the martyr Khaled Said Old Atguetl of torture and beatings in the street in Alexandria June 2010. Spontaneous invitation was not planned from any political power or popularity. After the call is published by the events of Tunisia and encouraged all Egyptians to demand participation and dissemination of the idea. Page does not follow any party or group or movement or association Valsafhh stand-alone and do not support a person or idea is for all Egyptians who want to defend their rights. The page is based on self-efforts of members of the Page affection was the secret of their success.

Why pretend?

Egypt passed one of the worst stages of interest in all respects. Setting aside the reports cited by the Egyptian government to beautify the image but unfortunately the reality is different from those reports. Nzllona and all on 25 is the beginning of the end, the end of each silence and contentment and submission of what is happening in our country and the beginning of a new page of the positive and claim rights. On 25 January is not the sense of revolution is a revolution but a coup against the government to tell them we are beginning to concern the affairs of each other and we will take all our rights will not be silent anymore.

There are 30 million Egyptians depressives and text, including one million patients with serious depression and more than one hundred thousand suicide attempt in 2009 resulted in the death of 5000 people. We have 48 million poor, including Two and a half million people living in extreme poverty. We have 12 million Egyptians without any shelter, and a half million of them living in cemeteries.

There is systematic corruption led to the existence of corruption cases worth more than all of us more than 39 billion pounds in one year only. Egypt occupies

Position 115 out of 139 countries in the World Competitiveness Report of the Worlds, where government corruption.

There are more than 3 million young people unemployed and the unemployment rate among young people more than 30% and Egypt occupies the last place among 139 countries in the rate of transparency in recruitment.

We have the highest rate of child mortality in the world by fifty children per 1000 births. Egypt and a half children are infected with anemia and almost 8 million people infected with C. We have more than 100 thousand patients with cancer annually due to water pollution. Dita and ambulance per 35 thousand inhabitants.

Egypt's emergency law has caused the deaths of scores of Egyptians against torture and the arrest of thousands of them without any legal basis to arrest them. Because of the use of security for political control and abortion activity has resulted in a flagrant fraud in the elections of parliament that led to the ruling party gets more than ninety percent of the seats in the Council.

To learn more and the sources of this information, please watch this video.

Why on January 25?

In 1952 our forefathers resisted the police with their guns in the regular British army tanks and armies martyred, including 50 families and more than 100 and beat the finest examples of sacrifice for the nation. We are after more than fifty years now suffer from the practices of the police service which has become a tool to humiliate and torture the Egyptians. We chose this particular day because it symbolizes the fusion of the police with the people and this is what we hope on the demonstration that attach to the officers respected us because our cause is one. On 25 January is an official holiday, giving all Egyptians to participate without disrupting their business.

What are our demands?

The first requirement: Confronting the problem of poverty before they explode and that respect the rule of the Egyptian judiciary to increase the minimum wage increase in a fair, especially in the areas of health and education to improve services to the people. And to provide subsidies of up to 500 pounds per young university graduates can not get a job, for a specified period.

The second requirement: the state of emergency which caused the control of the security apparatus on Egypt and the arrest of opposition to government policies and put them in detention camps without any guilt. We call for the prosecution to impose control on the sections to stop the torture methodology that is practiced in police stations. And implementation of the provisions of the judiciary and respected by the Egyptian government.

Third requirement: dismissal of Interior Minister Habib el-Adli because of insecurity faced by Egypt represented in the incidents of terrorism and the proliferation of crimes that occurred at the hands of officers or members of the Ministry of the Interior without a strong deterrent.

 Fourth requirement: identification of no more than two consecutive terms, because absolute power corrupts and that there is no developed country to allow the president to stay in office for decades. It is our right to choose our president and our right not to fret a power judgeth the country until he dies.

Of course there are many demands for all Egyptians in the areas of health, education, uniforms and the beginning is that we are moving with some of the demand we demand through pressure on the government as a people, our affection, we draw the government and Nhasabha on their performance and identify priorities not vice versa.
Places and the timing of the demonstrations

Is very important that we understand that the goal of the demonstration is that we mobilize all the people Maana. People are all upset and wronged Omh satisfied if the country remains necessary to encourage them to participate and Ashan like this we want the work marches in all the areas popular with some people down in the marches of ten people Aktar reduce de place of the demonstration is very important. By the way places of demonstrations not limited to the places mentioned here because in places where demonstrations Tanih unannounced and Hatniz the demonstrations in different provinces. It is important that you come down and express your opinion and your anger is estimated by the Old way.

Greater Cairo

Duran Shubra

Turnover rain

AWAY WITH THE GATEKEEPERS

In front of Cairo University

Street League of Arab States

Important notes: the third-party organization demonstrations and marches in the popular neighborhoods in all parts of Cairo, Giza, Helwan, if you are in the popular area down on 25 January and joined to the matter.

Alexandria: two places have been identified for pause: the first place is the field station of Egypt and second place is the field Mansheya. To move all of the marches from all regions of Alexandria Corniche or going through the side streets so as to reach to the assembly points in the timing of the demonstration exactly. The other demonstrations will emerge from the premises unannounced For details contact on hills after 9 am on the phone: 01521543978

Ismailia: Thalathini Street and Railroad Street next to Hamzawy - call link on Facebook in Ismailia

Fayoum: the march of the great people of Fayoum will start from the field of epitopes Bandar Fayoum exactly two o'clock pm

Mahala: field-Bandar and field barns and the People's Republic and the assembly will be in fifth place will be announced in the demonstration

Tanta: in front of the conservative city of Tanta, assembly, the second time exactly

Sohag: the place will be determined on January 24 th Alatnen and follow-up information call link on Facebook in Sohag

Other locations: Please get off the bottom of the page and paragraph numbers to access interests to get the numbers, the coordinators of the demonstrations in your province.

Instructions to demonstrate

1) the demonstration was peaceful. We are advocates of peace and we are not advocates of violence. We demand our rights, and the first to preserve the rights of others. Will not respond to any attempts to provoke the security of Ashan us out of our Old and gets two Bejttoa guardian. Key goal of security objectives is to portray the protesters as we want the little thugs sabotage the country. Must show restraint and not recklessness and to do anything against the law or endangering the lives of any person to cause danger or damage to any property, public or private. In the case of the presence of any members of any violent act Baiqoumoua please bloc about the person and ruled out an immediate protest from within and to inform the security about it.

2) Please arrive at the place of the demonstration on time per minute. Delay causes the fragmentation of efforts and the potential failure of the demonstration. Presence at the same time makes it easy for the demonstration began and it is difficult for the opportunity to prevent security.

3) When you get out of the house do not carry anything you do not need such Karnahat or licenses or bank cards. I carry your ID and the amount is enough for any emergency. O rite Mottagabash your watch or need any break easily. Better be sporting uniforms or jeans with a jacket for protection from the cold in the case of the continuation of the demonstration or sit for a long time. O rite everyone answers Maah Gazzazh large water because it is within the demonstration Bacon is always in deficit in the water.

4) Please bring the Egyptian flag and not to bring any banners or signs to any particular party or movement, group or association or religious community. Today all we are all Egyptians to demand equal rights and social justice, we want the Omh disperse.

5) In the absence of any demonstrations Nzulk Do not be in the front rows and leave the front line to those who are more experienced to lead the march or demonstration Ashan Mihsalh messing up the March decision-making.

6) chants a unified and agreed. Please do not use any obscene words or engage in side battles with security personnel. Central Security is not your enemy. Is the soldier was forced during his service in the army to carry out this role in the case of non-obedience to orders is the most punishing sanctions. Try to focus as much as possible the feelings of anger towards the real enemy.

7) Try as much as possible not to disrupt traffic in the streets. We do not punish the citizens we demand our rights. Of course Batkelm for willful obstruction of the passage. Because in the case of the descent of tens of thousands in the streets of any traffic will be disabled Omh Dah Elly Bnteklm it.

8) March on your own .. I repeat, very important March alone because friends in the circumstances de Bivedoa. O rite be persuaded with a limit and your friend with some Tnzloa. Benninzel stadiums like what time of the Match.

Chants Standard

The idea of unified chants are the most important ideas to demonstrate. We all pitched to Egypt and we have to unite our ranks and we are one Ed. Henltzm with some cheers and all Henrkz on the issues of unemployment and poverty issues, because the de Old charges of all the Egyptians, Old Woody chants were agreed upon:

Long live Egypt .. Long live Egypt

Live .. Freedom .. Human dignity

Freedom .. Freedom .. Freedom .. Freedom

O freedom Fink Fink .. Emergency between us and you

Not Hnkhav not Hntati .. Hatred of the sound are we Allowati

O people of Tunisia Habib .. Shams not Htgab Revolution

With our blood .. We sacrifice ourselves for homeland

Lift your voice to say to the people .. We hatred of injustice salvation

One at least two .. We Egyptians

Healthy creatures shook the universe .. Egypt our country not Hthon

What the people of Tunisia .. The thief fled Madam

Minimum wage .. By the people as the whole arises

To see that my right to fill and I live .. And what Almlalim Petkvic

Egyptian night my healthy spirit .. Freedom of an open door

Come on you, the people fear Uday .. Lower the health of acetic Can See

The people of civilization and the glory years .. Not Hitati to the Day of Judgment

Telephones task

Communicate with lawyers

Numbers front to defend Egypt protesters, a group of lawyers who specialize in supporting the demonstrators and the preservation of their rights:

74

AWAY WITH THE GATEKEEPERS

0120624003 - 0129295510 to 0106701470

Communicate with the coordinators of the demonstrations

Greater Cairo: 0102864919-01521543977 - 0105805657 to 0123077912

Alexandria: 0182011578 - 0144584545 to 01521543978

Dakahlia: 01504665931 - 0172320006 to 01521543976

Aswan: 01521543979

Bank: 0119268243 - 0187606131 to 01521543982

Ismailia: 0103977677 to 01521543984

Port Said: 0104496590 to 01521921386

Assiut: 0144373186

Sohag: 0187627090 & 0177740064

Beni Suef: 01521543983

Suez: 01521921385

Red Sea: 01512934066

Qaliubiya: 01521921380

East: 01521543981

Qena and Luxor: 01521543980

Links of interest you

We are all Khaled Said Page on the Internet

Home Call for Revolution Day on corruption, unemployment, injustice and torture

Invitation PAUSE lawyers Egypt to protect the participants in the demonstrations

Front to defend protesters Egypt

Taking part in the demonstrations

Must be noted that greater involvement in these demonstrations will be one of the Egyptian masses is not interested in politics. Because the call and connection I felt their problems and tragedies. For this, the call came out from the ground up is politicized and came out of the page "We are all Khaled Said," which do not follow any parties or movements with a political objective. Has responded to the call on all political forces, because the demands, and because one of these political forces has mainly to defend the rights of the Egyptians.

April 6 Youth Movement

Grass-roots campaign to support the demands for change

Ghad Party

Youth for Justice and Freedom

Muslim Brotherhood

Wafd Party

The movement of a crowd

Democratic Front Party

ElBaradei's Association to support the demands for change

Al-Karama

Campaign support Hamdeen Sabahi

SRs

Dr. Mohamed Beltagy

Mr. Alaa Aswani

Mother of the martyr Khaled Said

Satirical writer Belal Fadl

Chancellor Mahmoud Khudairi

Artist Amr Waked

Director Mohamed Diab

Khaled Abu Naga

Appendix E: 198 Nonviolent Weapons

This appendix features figures the nonviolent weapons as outlined by Gene Sharp in his book *From Dictatorship to Democracy*.

Formal Statements
1. Public Speeches
2. Letters of opposition or support
3. Declarations by organizations and institutions
4. Signed public statements
5. Declarations of indictment and intention
6. Group or mass petitions

Communications with a Wider Audience
7. Slogans, caricatures, and symbols
8. Banners, posters, displayed communications
9. Leaflets, pamphlets, and books
10. Newspapers and journals
11. Records, radio, and television
12. Skywriting and earthwriting

Group Representations
13. Deputations
14. Mock awards
15. Group lobbying
16. Picketing
17. Mock elections

Symbolic Public Acts
18. Displays of flags and symbolic colors
19. Wearing of symbols
20. Prayer and worship
21. Delivering symbolic objects
22. Protest disrobings
23. Destruction of own property
24. Symbolic lights
25. Displays of portraits
26. Paint as protest
27. New signs and names
28. Symbolic sounds
29. Symbolic reclamations
30. Rude gestures

Pressures on Individuals
31. "Haunting" officials
32. Taunting officials
33. Fraternization
34. Vigils

Drama and Music
35. Humorous skits and pranks
36. Performances of plays and music
37. Singing

Processions
38. Marches
39. Parades
40. Religious processions
41. Pilgrimages
42. Motorcades

Honoring the Dead
43. Political mourning
44. Mock funerals
45. Demonstrative funerals
46. Homage at burial places

Public Assemblies
47. Assemblies of protest or support
48. Protest meetings
49. Camouflaged meetings of protest
50. Teach-ins

Withdrawal and Renunciation
51. Walk-outs
52. Silence
53. Renouncing honors
54. Turning one's back

Ostracism of Persons
55. Social boycott
56. Selective social boycott
57. Lysistratic nonaction
58. Excommunication
59. Interdict

Noncooperation with Social Events, Customs, and Institutions
60. Suspension of social and sports activities
61. Boycott of social affairs
62. Student strike
63. Social disobedience
64. Withdrawal from social institutions

Withdrawal from the Social System
65. Stay-at-home

66. Total personal noncooperation
67. "Flight" of workers
68. Sanctuary
69. Collective disappearance
70. Protest emigration [*hijrat*]

Actions by Consumers

71. Consumers' boycott
72. Nonconsumption of boycotted goods
73. Policy of austerity
74. Rent withholding
75. Refusal to rent
76. National consumers' boycott
77. International consumers' boycott

Action by Workers and Producers

78. Workmen's boycott
79. Producers' boycott

Action by Middlemen

80. Suppliers' and handlers' boycott

Action by Owners and Management

81. Traders' boycott
82. Refusal to let or sell property
83. Lockout
84. Refusal of industrial assistance
85. Merchants' "general strike"

Action by Holders of Financial Resources

86. Withdrawal of bank deposits
87. Refusal to pay fees, dues, and assessments
88. Refusal to pay debts or interest
89. Severance of funds and credit
90. Revenue refusal
91. Refusal of a government's money

Action by Governments

92. Domestic embargo
93. Blacklisting of traders
94. International sellers' embargo
95. International buyers' embargo
96. International trade embargo

Symbolic Strikes

97. Protest strike
98. Quickie walkout (lightning strike)

Agricultural Strikes

99. Peasant strike
100. Farm Workers' strike

Strikes by Special Groups

101. Refusal of impressed labor
102. Prisoners' strike
103. Craft strike
104. Professional strike

Ordinary Industrial Strikes

105. Establishment strike
106. Industry strike
107. Sympathetic strike

Restricted Strikes

108. Detailed strike
109. Bumper strike
110. Slowdown strike
111. Working-to-rule strike
112. Reporting "sick" [sick-in]
113. Strike by resignation
114. Limited strike
115. Selective strike

Multi-industry Strikes

116. Generalized strike
117. General strike

Combination of Strikes and Economic Closures

118. *Hartal*
119. Economic shutdown

Rejection of Authority

120. Withholding or withdrawal of allegiance
121. Refusal of public support
122. Literature and speeches advocating resistance

Citizens' Noncooperation with Government

123. Boycott of legislative bodies
124. Boycott of elections
125. Boycott of government employment and positions
126. Boycott of government depts., agencies, and other bodies
127. Withdrawal from government educational institutions
128. Boycott of government-supported organizations
129. Refusal of assistance to enforcement agents
130. Removal of own signs and

placemarks
131. Refusal to accept appointed officials
132. Refusal to dissolve existing institutions
133. Reluctant and slow compliance
134. Nonobedience in absence of direct supervision
135. Popular nonobedience
136. Disguised disobedience
137. Refusal of an assemblage or meeting to disperse
138. Sit-down
139. Noncooperation with conscription and deportation
140. Hiding, escape, and false identities
141. Civil disobedience of "illegitimate" laws

Action by Government Personnel
142. Selective refusal of assistance by government aides
143. Blocking of lines of command and information
144. Stalling and obstruction
145. General administrative noncooperation
146. Judicial noncooperation
147. Deliberate inefficiency and selective noncooperation by enforcement agents
148. Mutiny

Domestic Governmental Action
149. Quasi-legal evasions and delays
150. Noncooperation by constituent governmental units

International Governmental Action
151. Changes in diplomatic and other representations
152. Delay and cancellation of diplomatic events
153. Withholding of diplomatic recognition
154. Severance of diplomatic relations
155. Withdrawal from international organizations
156. Refusal of membership in international bodies
157. Expulsion from international organizations

Psychological Intervention
158. Self-exposure to the elements
159. The fast
   a) Fast of moral pressure
   b) Hunger strike
   c) Satyagrahic fast
160. Reverse trial
161. Nonviolent harassment

Physical Intervention
162. Sit-in
163. Stand-in
164. Ride-in
165. Wade-in
166. Mill-in
167. Pray-in
168. Nonviolent raids
169. Nonviolent air raids
170. Nonviolent invasion
171. Nonviolent interjection
172. Nonviolent obstruction
173. Nonviolent occupation

Social Intervention
174. Establishing new social patterns
175. Overloading of facilities
176. Stall-in
177. Speak-in
178. Guerrilla theater
179. Alternative social institutions
180. Alternative communication systems

Economic Intervention
181. Reverse strike
182. Stay-in strike
183. Nonviolent land seizure
184. Defiance of blockades
185. Politically motivated counterfeiting
186. Preclusive purchasing
187. Seizure of assets
188. Dumping
189. Selective patronage
190. Alternative markets
191. Alternative transportation systems
192. Alternative economic institutions

Political Intervention

193. Overloading of administrative systems
194. Disclosing identities of secret agents
195. Seeking imprisonment
196. Civil disobedience of "neutral" laws
197. Work-on without collaboration
198. Dual sovereignty and parallel government

Appendix F: Blueprint of Social Media and the 2011 Egyptian Revolution

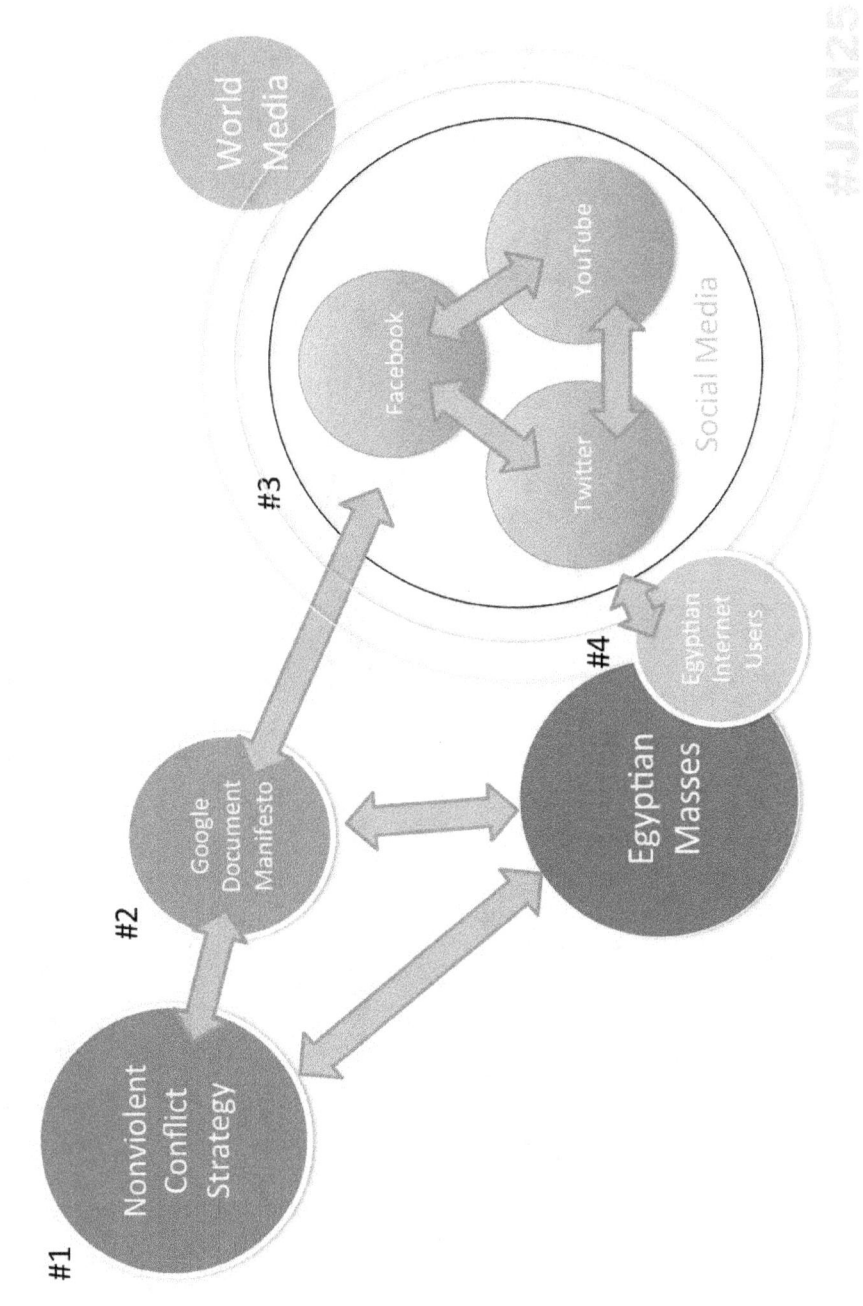

Appendix G: Channeling negative sentiment into action

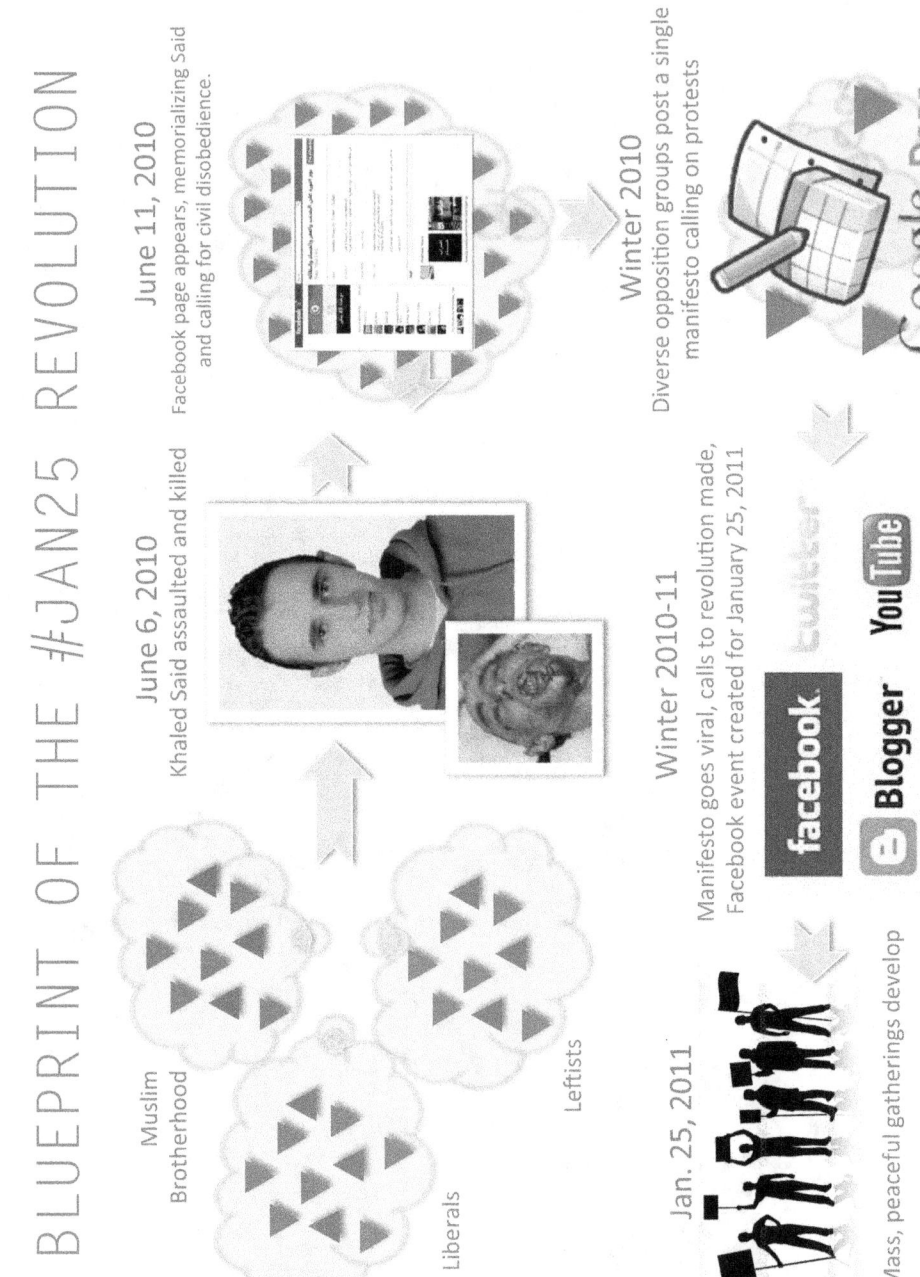

BLUEPRINT OF THE #JAN25 REVOLUTION

June 11, 2010
Facebook page appears, memorializing Said and calling for civil disobedience.

Winter 2010
Diverse opposition groups post a single manifesto calling on protests

June 6, 2010
Khaled Said assaulted and killed

Muslim Brotherhood

Liberals

Leftists

Winter 2010-11
Manifesto goes viral, calls to revolution made, Facebook event created for January 25, 2011

Jan. 25, 2011
Mass, peaceful gatherings develop

The Tweet Heard Around the World: The Growing Influence of the Multinational New Media Industry in International Relations

"A man bled to death on a street in Tehran on Monday. As one bystander tenderly held his head, five others held out their cameras," reported Paul Richter and Brian Stelter on June 19, 2009 as they covered the ongoing unrest in Iran's capital, Tehran. This graphic scene may have only reached the outside world as black and white letters on paper only a decade ago, but today, ordinary citizens with digital technology are able to broadcast graphic written reports, photos, and video that may instantly reach Internet users around the globe in minutes with great effect, whether intended or not. The confluence of communication technology and non-state actors, such as demonstrators, non-governmental organizations, terrorists, criminals, and a whole slew of other characters means that conflict in the modern world is increasingly broadcast in real time to the connected world. Whereas governments and traditional media outlets have exercised a monopoly on everything from satellite imagery to television shows in the past, an often anarchic surge in so-called New Media (blogs, photo sharing, text messaging, video sharing, etc.) is increasingly proving its ability to influence international relations and test state power.

By pure coincidence, New Media was born right as the United States was entering the War on Terror. But unlike the open media briefs given by U.S. Army General Normal Schwarzkopf during the Gulf War or the almost embarrassing media coverage of U.S. Marines landing in Somalia to waiting television crews, Operation Enduring Freedom was virtually sealed from the international media. In 2001, New York Times journalist

Michael R. Gordon reported "…media's access to American military operations is more far more limited than in any recent conflict, including NATO's war against Yugoslavia, the American invasion of Haiti or the American intervention in Somalia." According to Gordon, the military preferred absolute control over its message, using websites like defenslink.mil and video produced by military public affairs teams. Considering Afghanistan's wrecked infrastructure and lack of internet connectivity, there were few, if any, New Media outlets reporting during the American invasion there. However, two years later, New Media covering Operation Iraqi Freedom would prove much more prolific and difficult to control.

In an attempt to incorporate journalists into the 2003 invasion of Iraq, Secretary of Defense Donald Rumsfeld allowed journalists to be embedded into military units, with the understanding that journalists had to conform to military rules, such as refraining from reporting on the exact nature of operations, the specific equipment used, and submit to blackouts should the unit commander deem them necessary (n.a., 2003). There was some concern that embedded journalists would lose their independence as a result. However, New Media allowed Iraqis living in Baghdad with an Internet connection to report independently of traditional media, something soldiers themselves would increasingly do later.

While the U.S. military and its embedded journalists were the primary source of news information about Operation Iraqi Freedom in the West, New Media allowed Iraqis to cover events from their perspective. In 2003, the BBC reported that a 29-year-old blogger writing under the pseudonym "Salam Pax" had been providing an alternative to Western media with their travel and reporting restrictions. Salam Pax reported about the

Shia reaction to U.S. occupying forces in Baghdad, as well as rumors that the United Nations and NGOs operating in Iraq were under U.S. pressure not to report the numbers of civilian casualties during the invasion. Indeed, Salam Pax was able to write openly about civilian casualties without restriction and without any allegiance to a media network or government. Almost instantly, Salam Pax was giving interviews to the mainstream press – interviews that carried the authority of local knowledge. Pax's influence – which extended from The New York Times to Arab media, led Peter Maass (2003) to proclaim him the "Anne Frank of the war." While this may seem like one Iraqi lucky enough to have an Internet connection and global following, it marked the next stage of New Media in a post 9-11 world. Dozens of Iraqis began blogging independently of Western cultural bias or the reporting restrictions placed on embedded reporters.

While blogs were the earliest tool of New Media as Operation Iraqi Freedom began, New Media has since expanded into video, Google Earth, voice-over-IP, photo sharing, Facebook, and micro blogging "tweets." Each one of these rapidly developing technologies has made it increasingly difficult to control official messages. When considered as a whole – or "cloud," New Media's capacity to circumvent traditional information structures with real consequences for international relations is being demonstrated with increasing frequency. Even seemingly inconsequential issues can now have a chilling effect on policy when captured on New Media and distributed over the Internet literally millions of times. YouTube videos are especially influential in magnifying incidents.

In March 2008, National Public Radio published a report about two Marines in Iraq who videotaped themselves tossing a puppy over a cliff, with the puppy presumably suffering. Even though the U.S. government had held journalists under strict reporting rules, New Media and the ease in which it spreads worldwide meant that the video posted by aloof Marines on YouTube created an especially damaging situation that offended Americans and others alike. Even though massive human suffering was taking place in Iraq, the "puppy toss" became a public relations nightmare for the U.S. military (as it seemed to support critics' argument that the occupation was inherently cruel). Other incidents such as the Abu Ghraib scandal were captured with the tools of New Media – digital cameras – and spread within seconds across the globe once they were released. As a consequence, the United States was condemned and suffered a major diplomatic setback. Because of so-called "YouTube moments," blogs, and digital images, the United States lost political capital in Iraq that it may not have lost on previous conflicts where traditional media prevailed.

State security at home and abroad may also be eroded by New Media, while non-state actors may be empowered. Although many staples of New Media like the satellite imaging service Google Earth are meant to spread knowledge benevolently, there are emerging examples of the service being used by non-state actors to carry out attacks. In 2007, The Guardian journalists Clancy Chassey and Bobby Johnson interviewed an Al-Aqsa rocket unit commander in Gaza who explained how he used Google Earth to gather targeting data for targets in Israel. Indeed, the commander, on camera, demonstrated the 3D modeling capability he used for targeting. Perhaps worried about a similar terrorist threat in Britain, Scotland Yard has expressed deep concerns over the new Google Street View service, which may allow terrorists or criminals to rehearse operations without ever being on-site before (Independent, 2009). In another example, Google Earth fans have collaborated to catalogue North Korean military, civil, and government sites with Central Intelligence Agency-like professionalism. In future conflicts, patriotic Internet users may collectively interpret Google satellite imagery to support their cause, reports Evan Ramstad of The Wall Street Journal (2009).

However, New Media is playing a larger, more visible role in helping groups communicate in general. Perhaps the most current example of New Media undermining government authority is in Iran. Following the much contested presidential election results on June 13, 2009, opposition groups used Facebook to communicate and coordinate demonstrations more efficiently (as Facebook is able to quickly disseminate information among social groups), the messaging service Twitter to send short text updates to followers, Flickr to post in near real time photos of police brutality and blood-stained students, and YouTube to spread propaganda with the dramatic images blended with Iranian music (MSNBC, 2009). The seeming perfect storm of New Media involved in the Iranian unrest was so influential that the U.S. State Department requested Twitter delay any system maintenance that would interrupt the Iranians' ability to communicate via the service (MSNBC, 2009). Indeed, MSNBC reported that Iran's inability to control digital media leaks may have forced the Iranian government to employ Twitter to tell its own version of the story. In any case, the Iranian example shows the latest, perhaps most potent example of New Media's creeping power. While Iran accuses the West of meddling in Iran's internal affairs through a cyber war, other closed societies may be taking copious notes as they ready their information security and surveillance plans to counter New Media.

New Media is not invincible, however. Indeed, China has been able to create a "Great Firewall" staffed by, the U.S. State Department estimates, around 50,000 censors (Council on Foreign Relations, 2008). In a move similar to the U.S. military's initiative to incorporate embedded journalists during the Iraq invasion as to gain some control over the media, China has incorporated some multinational New Media providers into its censorship apparatus in exchange for access to its markets. The Council of Foreign Relations reports that U.S. companies such as Google, Microsoft, and Yahoo! are actively cooperating with Chinese censors and providing software to enable the suppression of illegal political information. Access to websites like YouTube, Flickr, Facebook, Twitter, and others is frequently and unexplainably denied. Even ordinary access is filtered for politically sensitive information, suggesting that New Media does have its limits, especially when multinational New Media corporations, like Google, have vested interests in the host state (CFR, 2008). Currently, New Media poses the greatest threat to weak or transitional governments seeking to suppress information.

While New Media and the multinational corporations that administer it may be limited in areas of strong, organized state suppression, the fact remains that – like newspapers 50 years ago – New Media is becoming a ubiquitous, legitimate form of communication with an inherent, dual-use potential. Just as illegal printing presses in Communist Poland were used to distribute anti-government Solidarity propaganda, blogs may be used to discuss pop stars or call masses to protest; YouTube may be used to promote the latest iPod or a cell phone video showing Egyptian police torturing a prisoner; Flickr may be used to share vacation photos, or feed the world massacre photos before CNN could ever get visas for its journalists; Twitter may be used to follow

Lindsay Lohan's every move, or call students to launch denial of service attacks on government websites. In each case, New Media is both incredibly dynamic and, some governments might posit, unpredictably dangerous. Except in those places, such as China, where the state can influence multinational New Media corporations like Google, New Media will continue to play an increasing role in facilitating popular resistance to oppressive governments and make public relations management, even in democratic societies, a much more demanding task. To what degree multinational New Media industry will erode state power is largely, it may seem, up to states and market forces to decide.

References

BBC. (2003, September 19). 'Baghdad blogger': Iraq not free. Retrieved June 20, 2009, from http://news.bbc.co.uk/2/hi/middle_east/3123172.stm

Chassay, C. & Johnson, B. (2007, October 25). Google Earth used to target Israel. The Guardian. Retrieved June 20, 2009, from http://www.guardian.co.uk/technology/2007/oct/25/google.israel

Council on Foreign Relations. (2008, March 18). Media censorship in China. Retrieved on June 20, 2009, from http://www.cfr.org/publication/11515/#6

Gordon, M. (2001, October 21). A nation challenged: the media; military is putting heavier limits on reporters' access. The New York Times. Retrieved June 20, 2009, from http://www.nytimes.com/2001/10/21/world/nation-challenged-media-military-putting-heavier-limits-reporters-access.html

Maass, P. (2003, June 2). Salam Pax is real. Slate. Retrieved June 20, 2009, from http://slate.msn.com/id/2083847   MSNBC. (2009, June 16). Battle for hearts — and screens — of the world. Retrieved June 20, 2009, from http://www.msnbc.msn.com/id/31387533/ns/ technology_and_science-tech_and_gadgets/

n.a. (2003, March 27). Pros and cons of embedded journalism. Retrieved June 20, 2009, from http://www.pbs.org/newshour/extra/features/jan-june03/embed_3-27.pdf   NPR. (2008, June 2). Puppy-toss video ignites the web. Retrieved June 20, 2009, from http://www.npr.org/templates/story/story.php?storyId=87913539

Ramstad, E. (2009, May 22). Gulags, nukes and a water slide: Citizen spies lift North Korea's veil. The   Wall Street Journal. Retrieved June 20, 2009, from http://online.wsj.com/article/SB124295017403345489.html

Richter, P. & Stelter, B. (2009, June 19). Twitter captures Iran's rebels. The Age. Retrieved June 20, 2009, from http://www.theage.com.au/world/twitter-captures-irans-rebels-20090618-clx3.html

The Independent. (2009, March 21). Public urged to report Google Street view fears. Retrieved June 20, 2009, from http://www.independent.co.uk/news/ media/online/public-urged-to-report-google-street-view-fears-1650832.html

ACKNOWLEDGEMENTS

For their assistance with this thesis, I would like to thank Professor Richard Shultz for his expertise and David Sussman for his persistence. For their excellent and always insightful counsel, I especially thank my fellow GMAPers Chris Allsup, Ian Rosenberger, Tyson Johnson, Dalia Ziada, Mark Mullinix, Jake Watson, Andrew Gordon, Pablo Rabczuk, and Enrique Alanis. I would also like to thank Patrick Meier, who was always willing to answer inquiries. Special thanks to Jason Hines of Recorded Future for his insights to predictive and automated social media exhaust analytics.

This thesis would not have been possible without the encouragement and assistance of Jimmy and Jennifer Bunn, Butch and Peggy Bunn, Tasha Pettis, Casey Kugler, Geoffrey Carter, Col. Todd Walsh, Maj. (P) John Moore, Roger Maynulet, Shane Goldberg, Jason Thompson, Michelle Watts, Kimberly Dannels-Ruff, Lindsey Ryan, Robert Hones, Stacey Moneymaker-Donachie, Col. Bill Huber, Paul Stuart, Todd Seitz, Dave McNally, Slade Walters, Lt. Col. Gene Warren, Assad Mizel, Tariq, Haider, Robert Myers, Brig. General David Fox, Kathleen Marin, Karl Weisel, Endri Misho, Safdar, Russell Wicke, Eric F. Cooke, Niraj Tamrakar, Michael Mesa, and many others. I would also like to thank Admiral James Stavridis and his staff for taking an interest in my thesis and nonviolent conflict. I would also like to thank the Fletcher School library staff and the Heidelberg University library staff in Germany. You have all inspired me more than you know.

Special thanks to Dr. Gene Sharp of the Albert Einstein Institute and Executive Director Jamila Raqib for their research and advancing freedom through the study of nonviolent struggle.

Most importantly, I want to thank my wife and best friend of more than 11 years, Nora, who I first met in this wonderful city of Boston. Her steadfast support, unconditional love, and patience have seen us through the lows of war to the highs of both finishing out master's degrees after traveling the world together.

Dr. Gene Sharp, Dalia Ziada, and Dan Thompson on July 20, 2012 in Boston.

www.ingramcontent.com/pod-product-compliance
Lightning Source LLC
Chambersburg PA
CBHW070550290526
45790CB00002B/620